FROM DILL TO DRACULA

A ROMANIAN FOOD & FOLKLORE COOKBOOK

A.M. RUGGIRELLO

ISBN: 978-1-7354200-0-4 (Hardcover)
ISBN: 978-1-7354200-2-8 (Electronic)
ISBN: 978-1-7354200-1-1 (Paperback)

Front cover shows *Sarmale* (Stuffed Cabbage Rolls); for recipe, see page 142.

Cover and book design by www.CardboardMonet.com.
Translation by Iuliana Marin.

First printing edition 2020.

www.FromDillToDracula.com

PUBLISHER'S NOTE

Although the advice and information in this book are believed to be accurate and true at the time of going to press, neither the author nor the publisher can accept any legal responsibility or liability for any errors or omissions that may be made nor for any inaccuracies nor for any harm or injury that comes about from following instructions or advice in this book.

To Romania,
a country as beautiful as she is strong.
Te iubesc

It's was a big plesure to work with you, and I know the life surprises us with new beginnings.
I wish all the best David. and to remain a pleasant memory in your heart.
Ana Moise (BARNSLEY HOUSE)

TABLE OF CONTENTS

ROCK SCULPTURE OF DECEBALUS ON THE RIVER DANUBE

INTRODUCERE *{introduction}*

First thing's first: I can't begin to express how grateful I am that you picked up my little Romanian cookbook in the sea of others. So, before we go any further on this journey together, I have one very important thing to say to you:

Mulțumesc
{Thank you}

This book has become a true labor of love, but let me go back to the beginning . . . I grew up a child of Romanian immigrants, the first of my family born in the U.S.A. Having left Romania during the height of communism's asphyxiating grip, the filter of which they viewed their country was covered in a film of grime, heartache and never-ending poverty. They moved to America to escape and found both amnesty and opportunity. Romania drifted into the past, a distant memory tarnished by Nicolae Ceaușescu and his regime. As a child, I wasn't taught Romanian because there was no need to use a language associated with a country I'd never develop a relationship with. Any mention of Romania was met with an unintended harsh tone and a curt explanation. Of course, this wasn't because I asked, but because of the struggles and difficulties I was responsible for conjuring with my question.

I grew up distant — both literally and figuratively — from Romania because my parents weren't willing to relive their traumatic childhood experiences. And I can't blame them. As I aged, I came to the realization that my parent's didn't hate Romania the country. Instead, they were a casualty of communism — human greed. Becoming an adult, I longed to reconnect with my roots, to uncover the beauty of a country best known for crippling oppression and the fictional Dracula (otherwise known as the very real Vlad Țepeș). I embarked on this cookbook with the hopes of outshining the negativity and, through it, offer a glimpse of a country often overlooked or otherwise shrouded in the paranormal, instead highlighting the beauty of its rich history and richer cuisine.

In writing this cookbook, I was taken on a journey through the land of my ancestors. I found the beauty behind the facade, the strength behind the pain. This is as much a cookbook as it is a love letter to Romania— from the foods I've grown up enjoying, to the truly magical landscape and customs that make it unique.

Romania may have never been my physical home, but it has found a special place in my heart and, through this cookbook, I hope it finds a place in yours, as well. ♥ *Ashley*

ALEEA MAGNOLIEI, BUCUREȘTI, ROMANIA

SĂPÂNȚA, ROMANIA

TRADIȚII *{tradition}*

CIMITIRUL VESEL

Hidden away in the small Romanian village of Săpânța lies a Merry Cemetery where over 800 gravestones are painted bright blue, and are covered in vibrant illustrations or inscribed with darkly humorous limericks of the deceased. One famous inscription reads:

Underneath this heavy cross
Lies my mother-in-law poor
Had she lived three days more
I would be here and she would read
You that are passing by
Try not to wake her up
For if she comes back home
She'll bite my head off
But I will act in the way
That she will not return
Stay here my dear
Mother-in-law.

MĂRȚIȘOR

Otherwise known as Little March, *Mărțișor* welcomes spring after a long winter, marked by the first of March. During this special time of year, friends and strangers exchange delicate twisted red and white strings, sometimes affixed with a little, lucky charm, called a *Martisoare*.

For many, spring is the season of new life — rebirth. In addition to marking the arrival of spring, this time of year is also celebrates Romanian's beloved women. Both Woman's Day and Mother's Day are celebrated between March 1ST and 9TH.

PAȘTI

Religious holidays play an important role in Romania's culture and tradition, the chiefest being *Pesce*, otherwise known as Easter. The rituals span multiple days, including flowers on Palm Sunday, painted eggs on Good Thursday, a Sunday dinner, and the appeasement of the ancient spirits on Monday.

Many European countries share the tradition of coloring eggs and knocking end-to-end together in a game to see whose egg remains the victor. But there are no painted eggs as beautiful as those made in Romania. Instead of simply dipped in dye, traditional Romanian Easter eggs are hand-painted with wax and vibrant colors in the most intricate of designs. You'll want to put them on display instead of eat them!

ROMANIAN FLAG

Romania's flag has gone through many iterations through its history. Now, the flag consists of three verticle bands in the colors cobalt blue, chrome yellow and vermillion red. The three stripes represent the three pieces to Romania, including Romania proper, Moldova, and Wallachia, the latter two joining the country in 1859 (with Transylvania later joining in 1918). Their colors hold significance aswell, with many historians believing the blue represents liberty, the yellow represents justice, and the red represents fraternity of the nation. A coat of arms appeared in the center of the vertical strips up until when the most recent and recognized flag was made official in 1989, commemorating the fall of Nicolae Ceaucescu, and with him, communism in Romania.

RUSALII

A celebration of Pentecost, *Rusalii* or the Decent of the Holy Spirit, is an important Romanian Orthodox holiday that begins in May and symbolizes 50 days after Easter and the beginning of the Church.

The holiday — though rooted in religious belief — has a mythical side. You might find some Romanian men dancing the *Calusarii* in their yards as a request for healing and protection, and to drive out the souls of the dead girls called the *Rusaliile* (also known as the *Iele* other times of the year—see page 22) can be driven away.

TRANSFĂGĂRĂȘAN ROAD, ROMANIA

ALTRINGEN, TIMIS COUNTY, ROMANIA

THE BALLAD OF THE MIORIȚA {the little ewe}

The ballad of the Miorița has been considered one of the most eloquent and impactful folk poems of Romania, with over 1,500 variants only found within Romania's borders alone. Conceived in Transylvania, the ballad summarizes many important beliefs its people hold, the strong connection between man and nature, and Romania's pastoral society.

It follows the simple story of three shepherds, a Moldavia, a Wallachia, and a Transylvania, tending to their herd in the hills. The Wallachian and Transylvanian shepherds devise a plot to murder the wealthier Moldovian and steal his herd, but his faithful, magical ewe — the ballad's namesake, the Miorița — learns of this plan and tries to prevent the murder. The conversation between the man and his beast is full of emotion. The Miorița begs the Moldovian to protect himself, but the shepherd doesn't feel the need to because he doesn't fear death, or even the knowledge of impending death. He's willing to accept that whatever happens is meant to happen.

But he knows he can't leave the world without first setting his affairs in order. The shepherd relays his final wishes to his ewe. Through the story of a hypothetical wedding, he describes how he wishes to be buried. The fall of the star marks both the end of his tale and his death, a metaphor transfiguring his wedding as a union with the vast cosmos from above, and contrast the wedding with the typical Romanian funeral customs, in a beautiful blend of subtle symbolism.

The Moldovian made the Miorița promise to share this story with his mother, who would certainly come looking for him, but to omit the mention of the falling star, leaving her to believe her son married went away to marry a princess.

You'll find the poem in its entirety on the following pages. It is often memorized and sung by school children.

THE MIORITA

Near a low foothill
At Heaven's doorsill,
Where the trail's descending
To the plain and ending,
Here three shepherds keep
Their three flocks of sheep,
One, Moldavian,
One, Transylvanian
And one, Vrancean.

Now, the Vrancean
And the Transylvanian
In their thoughts, conniving,
Have laid plans, contriving
At the close of day
To ambush and slay
The Moldavian;
He, the wealthier one,
Had more flocks to keep,
Handsome, long-horned sheep,
Horses, trained and sound,
And the fiercest hounds.

One small ewe-lamb, though,
Dappled gray as tow,
While three full days passed
Bleated loud and fast;
Would not touch the grass.
"Ewe-lamb, dapple-gray,
Muzzled black and gray,
While three full days passed
You bleat loud and fast;
Don't you like this grass?

Are you too sick to eat,
Little lamb so sweet?
"Oh my master dear,
Drive the flock out near
That field, dark to view,
Where the grass grows new,
Where there's shade for you.

"Master, master dear,
Call a large hound near,
A fierce one and fearless,
Strong, loyal and peerless.

The Transylvanian
And the Vrancean
When the daylight's through
Mean to murder you."

"Lamb, my little ewe,
If this omen's true,
If I'm doomed to death
On this tract of heath,
Tell the Vrancean
And Transylvanian
To let my bones lie
Somewhere here close by,
By the sheepfold here
So my flocks are near,
Back of my hut's grounds
So I'll hear my hounds.

Tell them what I say:
There, beside me lay

One small pipe of beech
With its soft, sweet speech,
One small pipe of bone
Whit its loving tone,
One of elder wood,
Fiery-tongued and good.

Then the winds that blow
Would play on them so
All my listening sheep
Would draw near and weep
Tears, no blood so deep.

How I met my death,
Tell them not a breath;
Say I could not tarry,
I have gone to marry
A princess – my bride
Is the whole world's pride.

At my wedding, tell
How a bright star fell,
Sun and moon came down
To hold my bridal crown,
Firs and maple trees
Were my guests; my priests
Were the mountains high;
Fiddlers, birds that fly,
All birds of the sky;
Torchlights, stars on high.

But if you see there,
Should you meet somewhere,
My old mother, little,
With her white wool girdle,
Eyes with their tears flowing,

Over the plains going,
Asking one and all,
Saying to them all,
"Who has ever known,
Who has seen my own
Shepherd fine to see,
Slim as a willow tree,
With his dear face, bright
As the milk-foam, white,
His small moustache, right
As the young wheat's ear,
With his hair so dear,
Like plumes of the crow
Little eyes that glow
Like the ripe black sloe?'

Ewe-lamb, small and pretty,
For her sake have pity,
Let it just be said
I have gone to wed
A princess most noble
There on Heaven's doorsill.

To that mother, old,
Let it not be told
That a star fell, bright,
For my bridal night;
Firs and maple trees
Were my guests, priests
Were the mountains high;
Fiddlers, birds that fly,
All birds of the sky;
Torchlights, stars on high.

BUCEȘ, ROMANIA

VLAD ȚEPEȘ III {Vlad the Impaler}

The one and only. The man who birthed both fictional and very real fear into the hearts of so many. When you think of Romania, I'm sure one of the first references to cross your mind is the infamous Vlad Țepeș, otherwise known as Vlad the Impaler.

It's true, his reign brought terror to the streets of Romania, but with it also came a level of safety and security, leading many Romanians even view him as a national hero, one of the most respected ruler of Wallachia. It was said a chest full of treasures and gold could be left in the middle of a village, and no one would attempt to steal it for fear of the wrath of Vlad.

{Symbol of the Order of the Dragon}

Bram Stoker based the character Dracula on Vlad Țepeș, down to the name itself. His father Vlad the II was a member of the Order of the Dragon, a monarchical chivalric established in 1408 by the King of Hungary, which gave him the title Vlad Draçul II. Therefore, his son took on a similar title, Vlad Draçul III. *Draçul*, in Romanian, translates to devil or dragon. It's easy to see how Bram Stoker evolved the title into the character of his novel, the namesake vampire, *Draçula*.

Dracula may be fictional, but his inspiration was a very real man. At Vlad the III's birth in 1431 in the Sighisoara Citadel, he wasn't evil. He was the son of Vlad II Dracul, who was viewed to be the illegitimate son of Mircea I of Wallachia, a Romanian hero known belovedly as Mircea the Brave. Vlad's childhood in the Saxon town of Sighișoara with his brothers Mircea and Radu was typical of Romanian royalty. When he turned 11 years of age, his life would forever change. His father refused to support the Ottoman Empire's invasion of Transylvania. Sultan Murad II ordered Vlad the II prove his loyalty and come to Gallipoli (Turkey). It's here where Vlad the III's story truly begins, because it's in Gallipoli where he and Radu became prisoners of the Ottoman Empire, hostages to secure their father's loyalty.

As prisoners, the Ottoman Empire worked to mold the two boys according to their culture and customs, hoping that when Vlad's time to take over the rulership of Wallachia, he would do so in favor of the Empire. While Radu developed a close relationship with the sultan, the opposite happened with Vlad, who developed a disgust and hatred for the Ottomans. He busied himself with combat training and became well-versed in the yataghan and the lance.

{Yataghan}

As his skills improved, so did his understanding of the Ottoman's brutality in war, with a special grudge against their cruelty toward his family.

He was released in 1447 following the death of his father and eldest brother. Their deaths are said to have been ordered by Iancu of Hunedoara, a Hungarian military and political figure who was the son of a Romanian noble family. With this knowledge, Vlad vowed that as ruler of Wallachia, he would exact revenge against those who wronged him and his family.

In this moment, and with everything leading up to it, Vlad the III became Vlad the Impaler.

He favored the art of impaling his enemies, a death that lingered, where victims might remain alive for several days at a time. Legend has it that Vlad would take meals beside the slowly dying bodies — his "forest" of spikes — sometimes including a chalice filled with the blood of his victims. A terrifying act of intimidation toward his enemies. The sight of all the impaled bodies was enough for the sultan and Ottoman Empire to coil back in fear. Historians claim hundreds of thousands of people were executed at the hands of Vlad through the ambush that led to his beheading in 1476.

History goes dark for much of his rule and life. It's believed he had at least two wives, with some claiming a third, and he had three legitimate sons whom he cared for dearly.

History and fiction may paint him as a monster, but he was also a man, one beloved by many.

MONASTERY ON LAKE, ROMANIA

BRAN CASTLE, TRANSYLVANIA, ROMANIA

FOLCLOR {folklore}

The *Strigoi*, or vampire, is no doubt synonymous with Romania in mainstream media, but they're certainly not the only stories passed down from generation to generation, through village and countryside.

BABELE {future prediction}

Not exactly a creature, but a time of the year. After a harsh winter, it's believed that the spring renewal has the ability to predict the future. This is likely rooted in farming activities, however as folklore tends to evolve through the generations, the concept of *Babele* has extended to personal aspects of people's lives. For instance, your happiness through the year is determined when you select a *Baba*, or a day that falls between March 1st and 9th. Based on the weather of your selected *Baba*, you can predict your future. Warm and sunny means happiness. Dark and cloudy means — as you might imagine — problems on the horizon.

A character by the name of *Dochia* is tied to this folklore, portrayed by an old (or, *baba*) and evil woman who insults the month of March. She met her demise when, after a streak of nine warm days in March, she mistook it for the end of winter, and went out without her coat. But, the weather shifted — as it tends to in March — and she and her sheep froze to death on a nearby mountain. It's said their ice forms became stone, and they are the "*Babele*" of the Bucegi Mountains, a southern part of the Carpathian mountain range.

CĂPCĂUN {ogre}

The *Căpcăun's* name translates directly to dog-head, but the creature is typically seen as an ogre with many exaggerated physical characteristics—extra eyes, extra limbs, and even eyes in the nape of their necks.

Regardless of appearance, the *Căpcăun* is believed to be a creature who kidnaps children and young women, primarily of royal origins. Many who have tried to rescue those captive have been met with unfortunate fates, as the *Căpcăun* has an arsenal of evil tricks to use against even the most honorable. If its cunning tricks happen to fail, their sheer size and strength is enough to strike anyone (or thing) down.

FĂT—FRUMOS {beautiful son}

Făt-Frumos is one of the greatest figures of Romanian folklore, an embodiment of the hero persona: a doer of good deeds and an aid to creatures in trouble. He can be found as the star of many Romanian stories, a role model for the children to love, and the conqueror of many of the malevolent creatures on these pages, as well as many others that continue to exist in fairytales.

IELE {fairies}

The *Iele* are known as The Ladies of the Wood, a mythical creature similar to the Nymphs and Dryads seen in Greek mythology. Some folklorists claim *Iele* are the souls of cursed women unable to find peace in the afterlife. Others believe them to be Dacian High Priestesses, the guardians of nature. These beautiful, fairy-like creatures come out of hiding at night, but I wouldn't spy on them if I were you, especially if you happen to catch them dancing. According to folklore, men have fallen mute or mutilated for life because they couldn't resist a peek (hence the need for men to dance the *Calusarii* for protection — see page 6).

Even though they aren't intentionally malevolent creatures, it is believed that everything they touch becomes dangerous.

POVESTEA CREAȚIEI {story of creation}
Every culture and religion has its interpretation of the creation of — *well* — everything!

In the Romanian beginning of beginnings, the land was covered in vast waters, known as *Apa Sâmbetei*. These waters were still as glass for as long as they existed, until one day the smallest of ripples appeared, as if someone breathed upon its surface. The ripple grew to become violent, bubbling waves. Foam churned off the water, and suddenly out of the foam a gigantic tree sprouted. On the tree existed a single butterfly and small worm. When the butterfly shed its wings, a young boy appeared. The worm went through a similar transformation, wiggling out of its body and another young boy appeared.

The second boy recognized the first as his *frate*, brother. But the first boy disagreed with the shake of his head, exclaiming, "You are not my brother, for I can have no equal. I shall call you Nonbrother."

TEREN {land}
Brother and Nonbrother, otherwise known by the names *Fîrtat* and *Nefîrtat*, went on to create the world together, starting with the vast seas. To create the land, Brother (who couldn't swim) commanded Nonbrother to dive to the bottom of the water and bring up the sand. After multiple failed attempts, unable to keep the sand from through Nonbrother's fingers, Brother collected the sand that remained beneath his fingernails, and that was used to create the land.

They placed the land beneath the tree they were both birthed from. Knowing Brother couldn't swim, an angry Nonbrother tried to drown him, pushing Brother across the waters in every diraction as he slept. But, wherever Brother rolled, land appeared beneath. The harder Nonbrother tried, pushing Brother all across the globe, the more land came to be.

When Brother awoke, he saw the land spread too far and wide across the Earth. Using their strength, Brother and Nonbrother worked together to push the land together, thus creating mountains and hill, lakes and caves, swamps and canyons.

CER {sky}

After marveling at what they had done, the two agreed upon what was missing: a sky. They separated the firmament from the waters below and, while perched on the highest branch of the gigantic tree, Brother hung the stars and their constellations in the sky, as if embroidering them in the canopy of night.

But Brother miscalculated the weight of all he added to the sky, and the land began to sink into the sea. Nonbrother saw this and dove into the waters, constructing four pillars from the ocean, held by four supporting sea creatures, and it successfully held the land in place.

VIAȚĂ {life}

After seeing all they had done, Brother and Nonbrother began to create. Brother used his powers to create all forms of man and being, plants that bloomed and bore fruit, all that was beautiful across the land.

Nonbrother, with his wild imagination, experimented creating giants and shape-shifters, and other strange beasts and monsters. Brother and Nonbother's creations existed in peace, but as time went on, evil fell upon the land, and a great war arose between the beings, and that's how life has existed since the beginning of time.

PRICOLICI {werewolf-vampire hybrid}

If you thought vampires were terrifying, the *Pricolici* expounds on that fear. Vile, murderous and violent men in life become *Pricolici* in death, and take on the form of a wolf to rise out of their graves at nightfall. Their streak of terror against the living continues, where they have been rumored to attack villages in packs.

The *Pricolici* have been linked to very real, abnormally large wolf attacks across the Romanian countryside. With the largest population of *canis lupus* in Europe, it's easy to see how and why this folklore has persisted through the generations

STRIGOI *{vampires}*

The *Strigoi* have gone on to influence both the mainstream vampire and werewolf mythos. They're creatures birthed from their death via disease, arising to walk the Earth once more, shapeshifting members who can render themselves invisible, and — most notably — have an insatiable thirst for the blood of the living.

Many Romanian traditions are meant to guard against the evils of the *Striogoi*, including cloves of garlic to ward them off, or handfuls of rice as a means of distraction. It's believed a *Striogoi's* impulse to stop in the middle of their hunt and count rice

(or beans, or anything small and in mass quantities) when thrown at their feet, leaving their victims with enough time to run away to safety. Now Sesame Street's Count von Count makes a lot more sense . . .

There's only one way to destroy a *Strigoi* once and for all: to burn the body, mix its ashes with water, and to have the afflicted family drink the concoction. (Don't worry, you won't find *that* recipe within this book.)

To this day, if a village suspects the dead will rise, they'll run a stake through the deceased's heart . . . superstitions die hard in Romania.

URIAȘ *{giants}*

There are several varieties of *Uriaș* based on the region to which they belong, but most share similar traits. The *Uriaș* are said to be the first creatures created (see the Story of Creation on page 23), with heads as large as mountains. Despite their intimidating size, they were friendly creatures and lived together in peace and harmony with the humans.

Then, one day, a disagreement birthed a terrible war between the races, prompting Brother to flood the Earth and start over. Much like the Biblical account of the flood, it is believed that Noah and his family (Genesis 5) were the only survivors.

But the *Uriaș* have not been forgotten. Their burial mounds are said to hold vast treasures and hordes of riches that can only be discovered on Christmas Eve, Easter, or St. George's Day, when magical, mysterious fires danced atop their graves.

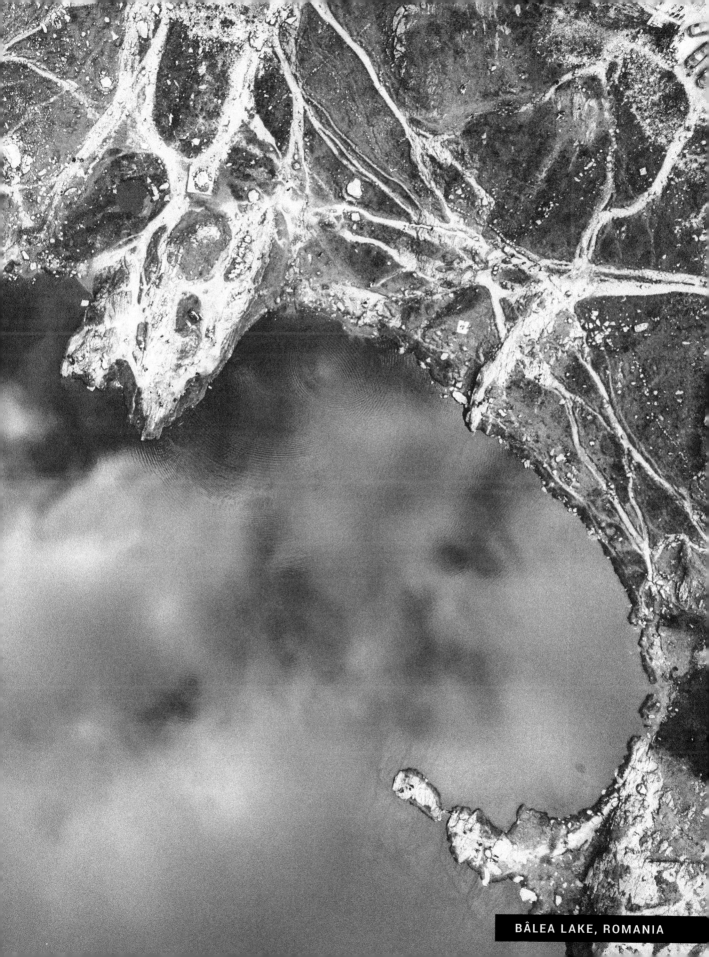

BÂLEA LAKE, ROMANIA

BUCĂTĂRIA ȘI INGREDIENTELE *{cuisine and ingredients}*

Romania's cuisine has been influenced by many outside sources. The seasons and seasonal harvests, in addition to religious tradition, factor into a recipe's popularity and can provide a deeper reason as to why it's being eaten during a specific time of the year. Symbolism plays a very important role in the ingredients used, from things like honey (*bees*) as a symbol of spring and new beginnings, to the intentional shape of a pastry meant to resemble the abstract human form.

But there's another *-ism* that has impacted Romanian cuisine: *communism*. Thanks to strict import laws and the surrounding powers limiting most — if not all — outside ingredients, Romanians were forced to utilize the land, what they could grow and nurture themselves, to feature in their dishes. However, not all foreign influences have had a negative impact. You'll find delicious hints of other cultures, from Turkey and Greece to more Slavic roots.

Food in Romania isn't created to simply offer nourishment (something it does, though, with a strong feature of the fruits and vegetables that are in season), but dining with friends, family, or even strangers serves as an uplifting, bonding experience, where bread is broken, stories swapped and laughs shared.

On the following pages, you'll find a short list of some of the most common — and beloved— ingredients featured in the recipes in this cookbook.

BRÂNZA *{cheese}*

Seen as a meal starter, both soft and hard cheeses are typically featured on a charcuterie board with different smoked meats and pickled vegetables. Not only is it common at the beginning of a meal, but it's utilized in many different ways as a meal finisher, otherwise known as dessert. *Papanași* (recipe on page 205) sees it as a fried topping to a deliciously fluffy donut and smothered in jam. Yum!

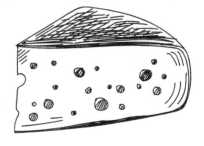

MĂMĂLIGĂ {polenta}

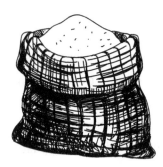

This staple of Romanian cuisine was once considered peasant food. Created from a simple ingredient, yellow maise flour, it can be featured as a breakfast, lunch, or dinner meal. It's commonly made in bulk, and poured directly on the family meal table for all to reach and enjoy. It can even be used as a bread replacement! If made as a stand-alone meal, you'll find this smooth and creamy porridge topped with your favorite smoked meats and strong cheeses.

Its versatility is unmatched in Romanian cuisine, and mămăligă can be layered, baked, rolled into a ball and fried, sweetened, etc . . .

MĂRAR {dill}

Part of this cookbook's namesake, dill is a beloved herb for most Romanians. You'll often find a dish topped off with the unmistakable flavor of fresh-cut dill, a compliment to the flavors of just about any savory Romanian recipe!

Dill can be used both as a seasoning and a preservative. When added to food, its volatile oils prevent fermentation and can extend the shelf life, which explains its use in pickling vegetables.

MERE {apples}

With an important job in both stews and desserts and everything in between, when it comes to Romania's plentiful and year-round fruit harvest, apples reign supreme. Whether you pluck and eat one straight from the tree, or leave it to simmer with cured meat, a few bay leaves, and plenty of paprika or garlic (more on both of those later), an apple can transform both itself, and a recipe.

PAPRICAȘ {paprika}

Paprika is a staple spice you'll find in every Romanian's kitchen, though that wasn't always the case. Indigenous to North and South America, it wasn't until Hungary (by way of Spain and Portugal) began to grow the chilies, and when the Ottoman wars battled over the Transylvanian region, that paprika made its way into the hearts and pantries of Romanians.

This brick-red spice will not only color your dish, but add a powerful explosion of flavor to it. From spicy, to sweet, to smoky, each flavor paprika brings has a special place in its own recipe. Unless otherwise specified, Hungarian paprika is most commonly used in the following recipes, however sweet paprika is a delicious alternative.

PORC {pork}

Pork reigns supreme as the most consumed protein in Romania, followed closely by chicken, and then beef (unlike many Western countries, where you'll find the opposite). Many Romanian recipes center around this beloved protein — sometimes it's mixed with another complimentary meat, other times it's utilized two ways in one dish (e.g. pork fried in pig fat).

Pork plays an especially important role during the Christmas season, where the rearing and then meal preparation from nose-to-tail is part of a village's customs and traditions.

Romanians love meat, but pork is absolutely king.

SMÂNTÂNĂ {sour cream}

Romanians put sour cream on any-and-every-thing. (Step aside *Frank's Red Hot*.) You'll find many of the recipes in this cookbook utilize sour cream, either as a crucial component to preparing a dough or as a finishing dollop on soups and — *yes* — even in sweet desserts. It's an ingredient that's easy for Romanians to create by leaving raw milk out for a day or two for the cream to separate and sour (thanks to its naturally-occurring bacteria), and voila! Romania's favorite condiment is born!

When added to your favorite stew, soup, side, or *sarmale* (page 142), it adds a creamy, cool depth and the perfect hint of sour you would have never realized was missing otherwise.

USTUROI {garlic}

Step aside, Dracula! Many of these Romanian dishes would cause a vampire to coil away in fear. If a recipe calls for garlic, you won't find less than three cloves — and you'll never be questioned if you choose to throw an extra clove or two in. (Actually, it's highly encouraged.)

Garlic isn't just intended for cooking, though. The idea that garlic can protect people and homes from evil spirits has been passed down from generation to generation. Though it may not be realistic, garlic *is* known to cure sickness, from coughs to the common cold.

Romanians regard garlic as a magical ingredient, and you'll find a dish just doesn't taste like Romania without it . . . and *a lot* of it.

VARZĂ {cabbage}

Fresh or pickled, cabbage is plentiful on a Romanian farm, which translates directly to its usage in many Romanian recipes. Pickled cabbage is homemade in large barrels, and those pickled leaves are the important little packaging for a minced meat and rice mixture in one of the best interpretations of Eastern European cabbage rolls, called *sarmale* (page 142).

The young cabbage harvest takes place at the end of August, which tells Romanians that autumn is around the corner, and so are hearty stews and *sarmale*.

BRAN CASTLE, BRAN, ROMANIA

PELEȘ CASTLE, SINAIA, ROMANIA

CHEIE DE CARTEA *{book key}*

While reading through this cookbook you'll occasionally come across three symbols in addition to the recipes. They are as follows:

LET'S LEARN ROMANIAN . . .

A fun moment to dive deeper into a recipe and learn a little bit of the Romanian (and pronunciation) that goes along with it.

ACCORDING TO FOLKLORE . . .

As you've already read, Romania is steeped in folklore. Whenever you see the bat symbol, you can expect a nugget of folklore knowledge.

MÂNCARE FOR THOUGHT . . .

Or, Food For Thought, *in addition to the recipe, these tidbits are there to expand on how you can take advantage of the recipe in ways not necessarily specified in the instructions.*

You'll also find pages, tucked away between the recipes, called Featured Food/Beverage which, as the name divulges, features a very Romanian-specific delicacy or drink that just isn't practical to make yourself—but is absolutely worth knowing about and searching for to try and taste for yourself.

IMPERIAL MEASUREMENT ABBREVIATIONS . . .

T for tablespoon | **t** for teaspoon | **c** for cup | **oz** for ounces | **lbs** for pounds

BRAȘOV, ROMANIA

PÂINE ȘI SUPĂ

{bread & soup}

PÂINE DE ȚARĂ {country bread}

MAKES 24 SLICES

Across cultures, bread has become the cornerstone of a meal. It's not only delicious, but a utilitarian tool to sop up all the leftover sauces or soups that happens to evade the reach of your utensils. In the Romanian version, we mix flour with cornmeal to create a hearty yet moist texture, perfect to fulfill all your dipping needs!

3 T	shortening
3½ t	active dry yeast
2⅓ c	water
1 T	granulated sugar
2 t	kosher salt
5 c	all-purpose flour
1 c	yellow cornmeal

BEFORE BEGINNING THE RECIPE

Leave the shortening out until it softens, about an hour.

1. Combine yeast, ⅓ cup lukewarm water, and sugar in a large bowl or stand mixer and set aside for 5 minutes.

2. Add 2 more cups of lukewarm water, the softened shortening, salt and 2 cups all-purpose flour to the large bowl. Using a wooden spoon, or paddle attachment with your stand mixer, mix ingredients together until combined.

3. In a separate bowl, mix 2½ cups of all-purpose flour with the cup of cornmeal. When combined, add to the yeast mixture one cup at a time, fully combining before adding each subsequent cup. Continue to add additional flour/cornmeal mixture in ½ cup increments to the dough if it appears too sticky. Knead until elastic. Place formed ball into a greased bowl, cover with plastic wrap, and allow to rise in a warm part of your home until size has doubled, approximately 1 hour.

4. Grease a large, round cast-iron pan and dust with cornmeal. Roll ball of dough from the bowl onto a floured surface and knead for a few turns before moving to the cast-iron pan. Press dough evenly to the edges of the pan. Again, cover with plastic wrap and allow to rise in a warm spot until dough size has doubled, approximately 1 hour.

5. Before dough has completely risen, preheat oven to 350°F. Use a knife to carve an 'X' into the top of the rising dough, dust with cornmeal and bake for 50 to 55 minutes, or until toothpick test comes back clean.

6. Let bread sit for 10 minutes before removing from pan. Cool completely before enjoying.

MÂNCARE FOR THOUGHT . . .

Slather on some Zacuscă (page 95) or Salate de Vinete (page 92) for the perfect appetizer or addition to your dinner meal.

COVRIGI {pretzel}

MAKES 9 RINGS

If you're anything like me, you believe all bread should be replaced with pretzel bread. That's not to say there aren't some delicious other breads out there but, in my opinion, pretzel is far superior, not to mention incredibly versatile. And while it's entirely possible I might be biased, as far as pretzels go, Covrigi takes the cake—er . . . the dough? Crisp but chewy and covered in salt and poppyseed, if you didn't think all bread should be replaced with pretzel before, this recipe is sure to change your mind.

2 ¼ t	active dry yeast
1½ c	water
1 T	granulated sugar
4½ c	all-purpose flour
2 t	salt
2¾ T	unsalted butter
⅓ c	baking soda
1	egg yolk
	poppyseed
	sea salt flakes

1. In a stand mixing bowl, combine yeast, 1½ cup lukewarm water, and sugar. Set aside for 5 minutes. In another bowl, mix the flour and salt together.

2. Turn the mixer on low and add the melted butter to the bowl of yeast, water and sugar. In ¼ cup increments, begin to add the flour mixture to the yeast mixture and combine together, increasing the speed until the dough no longer sticks to the side of the bowl.

3. Place ball of dough into a greased bowl, cover with plastic wrap, and allow to rise in a warm spot until its size has doubled, approximately 1 hour.

4. Roll risen ball of dough from the bowl and onto a floured surface. Divide the dough into 9 equal, smaller balls by cutting the dough into thirds, and then the three new portions again into thirds.

5. Take one ball of dough and roll it with the palm of your hand against your floured surface until you have a rope approximately 12" long. Twist the rope on itself and then connect the two ends so you have a twisted ring of dough. Repeat with all remaining balls of dough.

6. Preheat oven to 400°F. Prepare a baking tray with parchment paper.

7. Fill a large pot with water and bring it to a boil. When it begins to boil, add the baking soda. In a small bowl beat one egg yolk with a tablespoon of water.

8. Carefully drop two twisted dough rings into the water and let cook for approximately 30 seconds. Dough will swell.

9. Remove from water and set onto the tray with parchment paper. Repeat with remaining twisted dough rings.

10. Brush beaten egg yolk onto the top of the dough and sprinkle with salt and poppyseed, or preferred toppings.

11. Bake for 15 minutes. Pretzel should be a crisp, brown color.

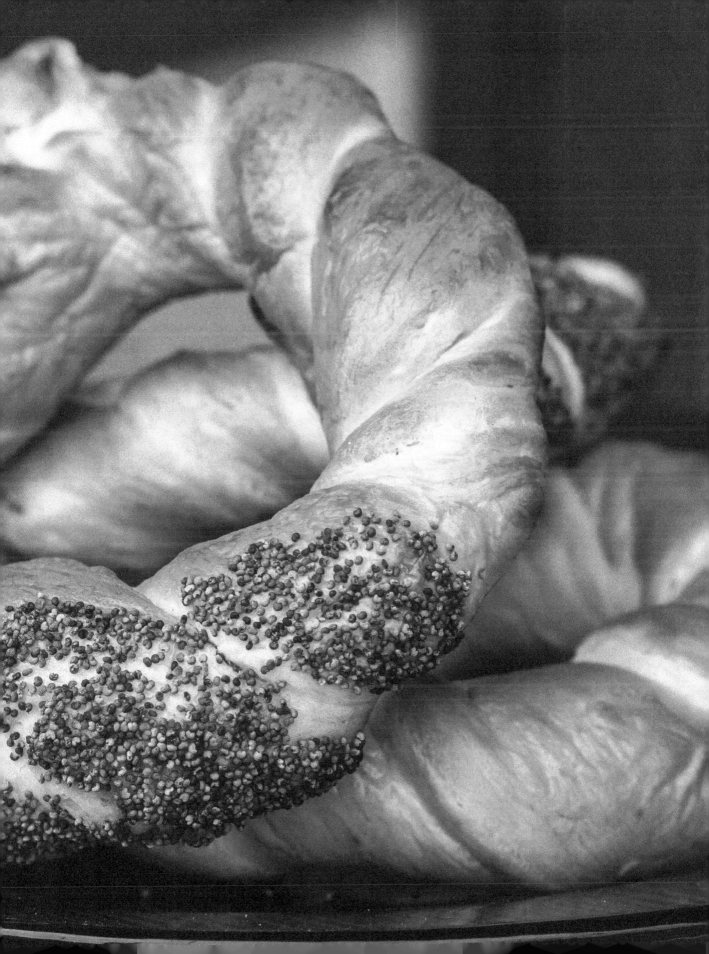

LÁNGOȘI CU BRÂNZĂ ȘI MARA {fried dough filled with feta cheese and dill}

MAKES 8

Lángoș *is a traditional dish that can be made sweet or savory, and—in a surprise twist no one saw coming given the size of the dessert section in this book—I actually prefer the savory version, hence the placement and variation of this recipe. You can find* Lángoș *in the north and northwest regions of Romania, heavily inspired by Hungarian cuisine.*

2¼ t	active dry yeast
1½ c	water
1 t	granulated sugar
4 c	all-purpose flour
½ t	kosher salt
1 c	vegetable oil
2 c	feta cheese
1	bunch of dill

1. Combine yeast, lukewarm water, and sugar in a small bowl and set aside for 5 minutes.

2. Add flour and salt to a stand mixer bowl and combine. Add in the yeast mixture and continue mixing for 5 minutes with a dough hook. Dough should become sticky and stretchy.

3. Place dough into a greased bowl, cover with plastic wrap, and allow to rise in a warm spot until size has doubled, approximately 1 hour.

4. Transfer the dough to a floured surface and divide it into 8 equal parts by cutting the dough in half, and the two new pieces into fourths. Roll each piece out so that it's approximately 4" in diameter. Add about ¼ cup of cheese to the very center, sprinkle with chopped dill, and fold the edges of the dough toward the center so that it covers the cheese.

5. Continue rolling the filled dough pocket until it reaches about 6" in diameter. It's okay if the cheese tries to escape from the dough (as cheese is wont to do).

6. Heat oil in a large frying pan and fry each individual patty until both sides become an even, golden brown, approximately 3 minutes per side, but be diligent about checking to make sure the dough doesn't burn.

7. Repeat until all patties have been fried.

8. *Lángoș* is best enjoyed warm with extra feta, large flake sea salt or chopped dill sprinkled on top.

SĂRĂȚELE CU BRÂNZĂ {cheese sticks}

MAKES 25 - 30 STICKS

Crisp and cheesy, and perfect as their own snack or as a carrier for one of the many dips you'll find further in this book. Unlike the traditional breadstick, sărățele cu brânză are neither crunchy or fluffy — they're flaky perfection!

4 c	flour
10½ T	butter
2½ c	grated Parmesan
6½ T	sour cream
2	eggs
1	egg yolk
1 T	milk
	large flake sea salt

1. In a large mixing bowl, add flour and butter cut into cubes. Mix with your hands until it resembles the consistency of sand.
2. Add in Parmesan, sour cream, and whole eggs. Continue to mix until well combined. Dough will become stiff. If still too crumbly, add water until you're able to form into a ball.
3. Wrap ball of dough with plastic wrap. Chill in the refrigerator for 1 hour.
4. Preheat oven to 350°F.
5. Remove dough from refrigerator and divide into 2 equal balls. Return one of the dough balls to the refrigerator while working with the first.
6. On a lightly floured surface, use a rolling pin to roll dough out until it's about ¼" thick.
7. Using a butter knife, cut the dough in half in one direction, and then in ½" strips in the opposite direction. You should end up with 13 to 15 strips per dough ball.
8. Twist each strip on itself a couple of times as you transfer them to a parchment paper lined baking sheet. Make sure the strips don't overlap.
9. Repeat steps 5 through 8 with remaining ball of dough.
10. Beat the egg yolk and milk together in a small bowl, and brush along the top of the sticks.
11. Sprinkle with salt and your favorite toppings, like poppyseed, sesame seed, caraway seed, etc . . .
12. Bake for 15 to 20 minutes, until sticks are an even golden brown.

TĂIȚEI CU OU {grated egg noodles}

MAKES ABOUT 6 CUPS

Growing up, my grandmother would cover her dining room table with these uncooked noodles as they dried. When that happened, you'd know where to find me: hiding under the table, trying to sneak a noodle, or two, or twenty — unsuccessfully, mind you — and in turn I'd receive a stern reprimanding for eating raw egg. (I do not condone consuming raw egg.) But it's one of my fondest childhood memories, and this homemade pasta now turns any sauce or soup into a bowl of joy. I hope you find that same joy through this recipe.

2	eggs
½ t	kosher salt
3 c	all-purpose flour

1. Beat together the egg and salt. In spoonful increments, add in the flour and continue to mix. Dough will become very stiff. Stop adding flour once this happens and the dough holds together but isn't too dry. Note: You may not end up using all the flour.
2. Once you're unable to continue kneading the dough in the bowl, transfer it to a floured surface and continue kneading for approximately 10 more minutes.
3. Finish by working the dough into a long, sausage-like cylinder. Cut it into 4 to 5 equal pieces. Leave out on the counter for them to air dry for a couple of hours.
4. When the pieces of dough have dried, use the large holes of a hand grater to grate the dough cylinders. They should grate to be about the size of a pea.
5. If the dough seems too soft when you try to grate it then you'll know hasn't dried for long enough. Leave it out for a few more hours and try again later.
6. As you grate, clear out the pastas so that they don't pile too high atop one another as they may stick together.
7. When all 4 or 5 pieces of dough cylinders have been grated, spread them across a sheet of parchment paper, either on a baking tray or on your counter, somewhere out of the way. Let pastas dry for an additional half hour before cooking. If you're planning on storing them for cooking at a later date, let the pastas dry overnight before storing in an airtight container and storing somewhere cool and dry.
8. As with most pastas, these will keep for a very long time when properly stored.

TO COOK IMMEDIATELY

1. Bring a pot of water to a boil, and cook noodles in ½ cup batches, as to not crowd them.
2. Cook until noodles are done to your liking, from 5 to 10 minutes. You can always pull them out when they're *al dente* and continue cooking in a sauce or soup, or sauté them with browned butter for a few minutes.

LĂSCUȚE {square pasta}

MAKES ABOUT 4 CUPS

Isn't it amazing how many different pasta shapes there are? They all boil down (no pun intended) to a few simple ingredients — water, flour and egg — and yet, the shape they're molded or cut into can make one variation taste better than another . . . I'm looking at you blue-boxed mac and cheese with various, delicious characters. As much as I love pasta in all its many forms, these squares may be my favorite. Given their dual-flat surfaces, they do hold onto their fair share of sauce or are the perfect size for a hearty and heart-warming soup.

1 c	all-purpose flour
4	eggs
½ t	kosher salt

1. Pile flour on your counter and carve out a small canyon in the very center. Break the eggs into this canyon and add the salt.
2. With a fork, begin to combine the eggs with the flour from the center of the pile and working your way out. Once most of the flour has been mixed with the beaten eggs, switch to using your hands to knead the dough. Dough will become thick. Continue kneading for approximately 10 minutes.
3. Form into a ball and wrap in plastic wrap. Chill in the refrigerator for 15 minutes.
4. Remove dough from refrigerator and divide into 2 equal balls. Return one of the dough balls to the refrigerator while working with the other.
5. On a floured surface, use a rolling pin to roll dough out until it becomes a very thin, rectangular sheet. Dust the dough with flour and set aside to dry while you repeat this step with the remaining dough ball. Dough should dry for a total of 30 minutes for each sheet.
6. After both sheets of dough have dried, cut it into four equal strips. Layer the 4 pieces on top of each other.
7. Cut layered dough into ¼" long strips, and then in the opposite direction, cut the strips into ¼" squares.
8. When all the dough has been used, spread the chicklets across a sheet of parchment paper, either on a baking tray or on your counter, somewhere out of the way. Let pastas dry overnight before storing in an airtight container, somewhere cool and dry.
9. As with most pastas, these will keep for a very long time when properly stored.

MÂNCARE FOR THOUGHT . . .

Lăscuțe are a great addition to any of the soup recipes to follow, whether or not they call for the addition of pasta (adding pasta is never a bad decision). I especially recommend adding pasta to my Supă de Fasole Transilvăneană (page 66) recipe.

GĂLUȘTE CU OU {egg dumplings}

MAKES ABOUT 5 CUPS

Similar to a German spätzle, *Găluște cu Ou are the perfect addition to a soup, sauce, or fried up on their own with mushrooms and onions (and I highly recommend you try that combination). It's a fuss-free batter that's easy to cook up — no drying time necessary!*

2	eggs
½ t	salt
¾ c	water
2 c	all-purpose flour

1. Bring salted water to a boil.
2. In a bowl, beat the eggs, salt and lukewarm water together until well-combined.
3. In ¼ cup increments, add flour to the egg mixture until the dough becomes thick and sticky, a cross between pancake batter and bread dough. If you happen to over flour the dough, add in water in ¼ cup increments. Set aside to rest for approximately 10 minutes.
4. In ½ cup increments, add dough to your *spätzle* maker, scraping the dough across its surface and through the grate holes. Let dough drop into the boiling water.
5. Occasionally stir to keep noodles from sticking together. Cook until the pastas begin to float to the surface.
6. Remove pasta from water with a strainer and serve in your favorite sauce or soup.

NOTE

This recipe requires a specialized tool to create the unique shape associated with the Găluște cu Ou, which you might recognize as being very similar to spätzle *from other cultures. You have quite a few options when purchasing this tool online, however this recipe recommends the one that looks like a cheese grater with a sliding tray attached to the top.*

PASTE CU NUCĂ {pasta with walnuts}

SERVES 8

The beauty of this recipe lies in its ease of cooking — utilizing packaged noodles — and its versatility of ingredients you likely already have your in pantry. As a child, our family traditionally made this pasta dish with crushed walnuts and sugar. However, many variations include additions like cheese, honey, raisins and cinnamon. Keep it simple, or get creative, either way, this unusual dish will surprise you in the best way possible.

12 oz	pasta noodles
3 oz	walnuts
4 T	unsalted butter
	granulated sugar
	to taste

1. Boil noodles according to the instructions on the packaging, or create your own noodles from my . *Tăițe cu Ou* (page 53), *Lășcuțe* (page 54) or *Găluște cu Ou* (page 57) recipes.

2. While noodles cook, grind walnuts in a food processor or spice grinder until it becomes a coarse powder.

3. Drain the noodles from the water (but don't rinse them) and mix in the butter and crushed walnuts.

4. Dust with sugar according to your personal preference.

NUDLI {potato pasta with bread and sugar}

SERVES 8

I know what you're thinking: Breadcrumbs and sugar? That's weird! *And, you'd be right. It is a bizarre combination, to be sure, but it also just . . . works. Think of them as a cross between Italian* gnocchi *and those frozen-aisle breakfast French toast sticks (the ones you know and love).*

2 lbs	russet potatoes
1½ c	plain breadcrumbs
¾ c	granulated sugar
3	eggs
2½ c	all-purpose flour
⅛ t	salt

24 HOURS BEFORE STARTING RECIPE:
Boil your russet potatoes for about 20 minutes or until fork tender. Store in refrigerator until ready to begin.

1. In a nonstick pan, brown your breadcrumbs until golden. Keep the heat on low and stir often, as the breadcrumbs have a tendency to burn. Allow to cool completely before mixing in sugar. Set aside.

2. Peel previously boiled potatoes and rice, either with a potato ricer or the ricing attachment with a device like a stand mixer.

3. In a large bowl, combine riced potato, eggs, flour, and salt, mixing to form a ball of dough. Add flour in ½ cup increments until dough becomes stiff. You may need more or less flour, depending on how much water your potatoes have absorbed. Continue kneading ingredients together until well-combined.

4. On a floured surface, roll out dough until approximately ¼" thick. Cut into long noodle strips, approximately ¼" to ½" wide. Length can be of your choosing, but they should be uniform for even cooking.

5. Gently drop noodles into boiling, salted water. Noodles are cooked when they begin to float, approximately 5 minutes. Drain and add to the breadcrumb and sugar mixture. Toss until the noodles are coated. Enjoy served warm.

MÂNCARE FOR THOUGHT . . .

This recipe can be served as a dinner entrée or a dessert, though we traditionally eat it as a side to some sort of protein, since they're sweet but not *that* sweet. *Unless you add more sugar, that is.*

SUPĂ DE GĂLUŞTE {chicken soup with dumplings}

SERVES 8

Supă de Găluşte *is the definition of comfort food. Between a Romanian homemade chicken stock, and dense, creamy dumplings, it's the perfect equation to warm the heart and the soul.*

FOR THE STOCK

1	whole chicken
⅛ t	salt
1 T	peppercorns
8	large carrots
4	parsnips
2	yellow onions
4	celery stalks
	water

FOR THE DUMPLINGS

2	eggs
⅛ t	salt
25½ T	Cream of Wheat®

FOR THE STOCK

1. Add chicken to a deep soup pot and cover with cold water. Let sit for 30 minutes.
2. Add salt and peppercorns, and begin to boil the chicken on a low flame for another 30 minutes. Simmer for 1 hour, skimming off the surface impurities as best as possible.
3. Chop your vegetables and add all but the carrots to the pot.
4. After another 30 minutes of simmering, remove the chicken and vegetables from the pot. Strain the liquid into another pot and let rest for 15 minutes.
5. Return the soup to your original pot by straining for a second time. Add the chopped carrots and bring back to a simmer for 15 minutes.
6. Remove carrots, and your stock is complete.

FOR THE DUMPLINGS

1. Add chicken stock to deep soup pot and bring to a light boil. Alternatively, if you haven't made your own stock you can use 10 cups of packaged chicken stock.
2. In a bowl, beat the eggs together with salt until they begin to froth.
3. Add Cream of Wheat® to the bowl, mixing to combine. Allow batter to thicken for 2 to 3 minutes.
4. Scoop up batter with a spoon to form a dumpling and gently drop into the boiling stock. Repeat until all batter has been used.
5. Cover the pot and simmer for about 15 minutes.
6. "Scare" (a very technical Romanian term) your dumplings by adding a ½ cup of cold water to the pot. Cover and continue simmering for another 15 minutes.
7. Add salt and pepper the soup to taste, and serve with a sprinkling of chopped parsley.

MÂNCARE FOR THOUGHT . . .

Don't let the chicken and vegetables go to waste! After simmering for so long, they're packed full of flavor and a delicacy all by themselves. My family would often fight as soon they're pulled from the broth! (Surprisingly, the celery was always a fan-favorite.)

SUPĂ DE SALATĂ VERDE {green lettuce soup}

SERVES 10

Quick and easy soups make for the best soups, and when all you need is a head of lettuce and some liquid, you have what I'd consider an easy soup. The cooked leaves don't offer this soup much in the way of density, but as soon as you add that spoonful (or two) of sour cream, it becomes creamy and comforting, perfect for a chilly winter day.

2	heads of green lettuce
1 T	unsalted butter
3	garlic cloves
3 T	all-purpose flour
1 c	heavy cream
8½ c	water
2	eggs
	salt to taste
	pepper to taste
	sour cream to taste

1. Wash lettuce leaves, cut into bite sized pieces and set aside.
2. In a deep soup pot, melt butter and sauté minced garlic. Add flour until it lightly browns, creating a roux, then quickly add in heavy cream and water. Season with salt and pepper to taste and bring to a boil. Allow to boil for 10 minutes.
3. In a small bowl, beat eggs.
4. After boiling for 10 minutes, stir in lettuce and cover until it has wilted. Then stir in the beaten eggs. Serve once egg has cooked through, approximately 1 minute.
5. Top with a dollop of sour cream mixed in and enjoy.

LET'S LEARN ROMANIAN . . .

As you flip through these soup recipes you'll notice some are marked as "supă" while others as "ciorbă." Both translate from Romanian to English as "soup," though they denote key differences between recipes.

"Supă" tends to refer to a sweeter soup with vegetables and/or noodles, but no meat, where as "Ciorbă" tends to refer to a more sour soup that contains meat along with vegetables and/or noodles.

SUPĂ DE FASOLE TRANSILVĂNEANĂ {Transylvanian bean soup}

SERVES 4

Contrary to what you might think, this soup is a staple of summer and not the bitter cold of winter. Take a second to let that sink in, and then enjoy the harmonious blend of hardy vegetables, warm broth and a nice, cold dollop of sour cream. Perfection!

2 lbs	wax beans
2	garlic cloves
1	yellow onion
1 T	unsalted butter
2	large carrots
2	celery stalks
2	large tomatoes
8 c	chicken stock
3 T	all-purpose flour
	salt to taste
	pepper to taste
	sour cream to taste

1. Rinsing wax beans, snap off the tails, and then break into bite-sized pieces, approximately 1" long.
2. Mince garlic and onions. Melt butter in a deep soup pot and sauté garlic and onions until tender, about 5 to 7 minutes.
3. While sautéing the garlic and onions, dice carrots and celery. Crush tomatoes separately and set aside for later.
4. Add chopped carrots and celery to the hot pan. Sauté for another 5 to 7 minutes.
5. Add chicken stock and wax beans to the pan, then salt and pepper to taste. Bring to a boil, stirring occasionally.
6. Once the soup starts to boil, throw in your tomatoes and reduce heat.
7. While the soup is stewing, pull out another smaller frying pan and make a roux by adding a ladle-full of cooking soup broth, and slowly whisking in 3 tablespoons of flour. Once the flour and liquid are combined, and develops a nice, light brown hue, add the roux to the soup and combine.
8. You can serve it topped off with a dollop of the traditional sour cream, and as with any Romanian soups, having a slice of bread to sop up the remaining liquid is a must!

SUPĂ DE USTUROI PRĂJIT {roasted garlic soup}

SERVES 4

You can never have too much garlic . . . right? If there's one thing Romanians love, and love to eat, it's garlic, hence a soup that makes it the star of the show with a whopping five heads of garlic! It's hard to resist eating the roasted cloves straight out of the oven. You house will be filled with the decadent aroma, and should keep even the most infamous vampires away!

5	garlic heads
4¼ c	water
2	large carrots
1	yellow onion
1	russet potato
2	celery stalks
1 T	unsalted butter
	salt to taste
	pepper to taste
	sour cream to taste
	sprig of parsley

1. Preheat the oven to 350°F.
2. Leave the garlic heads whole, but cut the tipped end off to expose the cloves to air. Roast on a baking tray for 30 to 60 minutes, until softened.
3. Bring water to a boil in a deep soup pot while chopping carrots, onion, potatoes and celery. Add to the pot and cook until vegetables are soft, approximately 30 minutes.
4. When garlic finishes baking, remove from oven and let cool. Once cooled, remove the cloves from the shell.
5. Add cooked vegetables, water, peeled garlic and butter to a blender and blend until soup becomes your desired consistency, either silky and smooth, or hearty and chunky. Season with salt and pepper to taste.
6. Serve with a dollop of sour cream and dusting of chopped parsley.

ACCORDING TO FOLKLORE . . .

Garlic is known for its healing properties, which could explain why a vampire wouldn't go anywhere near it—the undead are not exactly the picture of health, after all! Villages would distribute a clove during church service; a neighbor refusing to eat it revealed that while they walked among the living, they most definitely no longer were . . .

CIORBĂ DE FASOLE CU CIOLAN {bean soup with ham hocks}

SERVES 10

From the Ardeal region of Transylvania, prepare for a smoky soup that packs a punch in the flavor department. Every vegetable in your kitchen can go into this soup, and it leave plenty of room to get creative with the bean variations, too. The broth may be thin, but there's so much stuff in this soup that makes each spoonful dense and chunky.

8 c	water
1 lb	ham hock
1 T	unsalted butter
1	yellow onion
2	carrots
1	parsnip
1	bell pepper
3	celery stalks
4	garlic cloves
2 lbs	canned white beans
2 t	dried thyme
1	can of tomato paste
2 t	dried dill
½ t	kosher salt
½ t	black pepper
1	sprig of parsley
2	bay leaves
4 t	tarragon
	sour cream to taste

1. Add water (or vegetable stock, if preferred) and ham hock to a deep soup pot and begin heating.
2. In a medium skillet, melt butter and sauté chopped onions, carrots, parsnip, bell pepper, celery and garlic for approximately 10 minutes.
3. Add sautéed vegetables to the soup pot and bring to a boil.
4. Lower heat and add in beans, thyme, tomato paste, chopped dill, salt, pepper, bay leaves and chopped parsley.
5. Add tarragon to pot once the ham hock and beans are tender.
6. Continue cooking for 10 more minutes. Remove bay leaves before serving. Top with a dollop of sour cream and enjoy!

CIORBĂ DE PERIȘOARE *{meatball soup}*

SERVES 8

Pork meatballs bathe in a light and fresh vegetable-packed broth. With simple ingredients, but not skimping on flavor, it's a fantastic soup recipe to have on hand.

FOR MEATBALLS

1 lb	ground pork
1	egg
2 T	fresh dill
2 T	fresh parsley
¼ c	wild rice
¼ c	breadcrumbs
½ t	kosher salt
½ t	black pepper

FOR SOUP

2 T	extra virgin olive oil
1	yellow onion
2	large carrots
2	celery stalks
2 T	tomato paste
4 c	chicken broth
4 c	water
½ t	kosher salt
½ t	black pepper
½ t	Vegeta® seasoning
3 T	lemon juice
1	egg
	sprig of parsley

FOR MEATBALLS

1. Chop dill and parsley then add all ingredients together in a bowl and mix until well-combined. Form meatballs with approximately 2 tablespoons of mixture. Store meatballs in the refrigerator until ready to cook.

FOR SOUP

1. Heat olive oil in deep soup pot. Add chopped onions, carrot and celery, cooking until the onions are translucent.
2. Stir in tomato paste, chicken broth and water. Season with salt and pepper. Bring to a boil.
3. Add meatballs to the soup, cooking for another 10 minutes, until meatballs are cooked all the way through.
4. Add Vegeta® and lemon juice.
5. Beat the egg and stir into the soup. Cook until egg is cooked through, approximately 1 minute.
6. Garnish with a sprig of parsley and serve with sour cream..

MÂNCARE FOR THOUGHT . . .

Vegeta® is salt-based seasoning with dehydrated vegetable bits that helps to bring out the chicken broth flavor of soups. It's very popular in Eastern European cuisine, and is no doubt a pantry staple for any Romanian! You can find it at your favorite online retailers or turn to page 78 to make your own!

TOCANĂ DE CARTOFI CU CARNE DE PORC *{pork and potato stew}*

SERVES 10

Nothing warms the soul better than a thick and hearty stew filled with root vegetables that fall apart just as easily as the pork tenderloin. Stews are perfect on their own, or the perfect addition to pastas, rice, or mămăligă (page 111). The caraway, smoked paprika and hot sauce are the stars of this dish, and lend a spicy and smoky blend that the vegetables and pork soak right up.

6 T	vegetable oil
1 lb	pork tenderloin
1	yellow onion
1½ lb	baby potatoes
1	red bell pepper
2	large carrots
6 c	water
½ t	kosher salt
¼ t	black pepper
2 t	caraway seeds
2 t	smoked paprika
1 c	tomatoes
2 t	hot sauce
1	sprig of parsley
	sour cream to taste

1. Heat oil in a deep soup pot. Cut pork tenderloin into bite-sized pieces and add to the pot with the chopped onions. Cook until pork is lightly browned.
2. Cut baby potatoes in halves or quarters and add to the pot, cooking for 2 minutes.
3. Chop red bell pepper and carrots, and add to the pot, cooking for 2 minutes.
4. Add in water (or vegetable stock, if preferred), salt, pepper, caraway seeds, paprika. Continue cooking for 1 hour, or until pork and vegetables are tender.
5. Add in chopped tomatoes and hot sauce, garnish with sprig of parsley and serve with sour cream

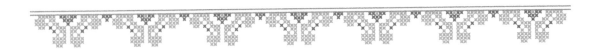

TOCANĂ DE MAZĂRE CU PUI {chicken and pea stew}

SERVES 6

When something is considered Romanian peasant food, that usually means the ingredients are simple, accessible, and can be easily transformed into something extraordinary. This recipe is common during the summer months, when fresh peas are abundant and the farms are bustling with poultry.

1 lb	chicken breast
2 T	unsalted butter
2	large carrots
2	yellow onions
2	garlic cloves
1 T	tomato paste
4 c	chicken stock
5 c	peas
1 t	Hungarian paprika
	salt to taste
	pepper to taste
	fresh dill to taste
	sour cream to taste

1. Cut chicken into large chunks.
2. Heat butter in a deep soup pot, and cook chicken until it has browned on the outside. Chicken does not need to be cooked through.
3. Chop the carrots, onions and garlic. Add to the chicken and cook until onions become translucent.
4. Add tomato paste and cook for 2 minutes.
5. Add chicken stock to the pot and bring to a low boil, cooking for 20 minutes.
6. Throw in the peas. They can be fresh or frozen.
7. Continue simmering until liquid has reduced by half and chicken is at an internal temperature of 165°. If liquid reduced too quickly, add more stock in ½ cup increments.
8. Season with paprika, salt and pepper, and serve with fresh chopped dill and sour cream.

MÂNCARE FOR THOUGHT . . .

Not feeling chicken? (Or don't have any on hand?) This recipe can easily be made with beef (Mazăre cu Vită) or pork (Mazăre cu Porc). Make it vegan by using tofu (Mazăre cu Soia) and replace the chicken stock with vegetable stock. The possibilities are endless!

VEGETA® DE CASĂ {homemade Vegeta®}

Popular in Eastern European cuisine, but largely unknown elsewhere, Vegeta® is a seasoning made of dehydrated vegetables and other more common herbs and spices. It isn't the easiest seasoning to find in stores, so here's a handy recipe to make your own!

10	carrots
5	parsnip
2	celery stalks
2	leeks
2	yellow onions
3 T	turmeric
2 T	garlic powder
2 T	dried parsley
6 T	iodized sea salt
3 T	black pepper

1. Preheat oven to 125°F.
2. Chop fresh vegetables.
3. Prepare a baking tray with parchment paper and dehydrate vegetables for several hours in the oven. Vegetables should be dry when removed from oven.
4. Pulse all ingredients in a food processor until a fine powder.
5. Store in an airtight jar or container at room temperature.

TRANSYLVANIA, ROMANIA

GRĂDINĂ

{garden}

CASTRAVEȚI COVĂSIȚI {pickles}

MAKES 5 WHOLE PICKLES OR 20 SPEARS

Why eat store-bought pickles, loaded with more sodium than anyone needs in a week — let alone a day — when you can make your own and control every ingredient that goes into it? And trust me, after tasting a homemade pickle, you'll never return to the super-salty jarred variety.

5	pickling cucumbers
1	head of garlic
1	mature dill plant
7½ t	kosher salt
1 T	peppercorns
10 c	water
1	slice of bread

1. Cut halfway through cucumbers the long way in one direction, rotate 90° and cut halfway through the opposite side.
2. Cut the bottom of the garlic head off, exposing the garlic to air, but keep it in its shell.
3. Add cucumbers, dill plant, garlic, salt, a handful of peppercorns, and lukewarm water to a large jar.
4. Add the slice of bread so that it floats on the top of the jar and cover with plastic wrap. Leave on the counter in the sun.
5. Remove slice of bread after 24-hours.
6. Check cucumbers daily, until they've become the pickles of your preference.

MÂNCARE FOR THOUGHT . . .

I'm sure you've noticed there's no vinegar in this recipe — not a drop. That's because we're making naturally fermented pickles. Adding vinegar prevents natural fermentation from occurring, which also means those beneficial probiotics aren't able to develop. Naturally fermented vegetables contain more nutrients and offer incredible benefits for digestion.

You're probably wondering how these become sour — a key characteristic of pickles — without vinegar . . . well, with just salt and water, a natural preservative, lactic acid is created when the bacteria lactobacilli *consumes the starches and sugars from both the cucumbers and the slice of bread. In the end, you get pickles with a whole plethora of health benefits!*

SALATĂ DE ROȘII
ROMÂNEASCĂ *{Romanian tomato salad}*

SERVES 4

Summer screams of bright and fresh ingredients that are quick and easy to fashion together in the perfect dish. As long as the tomatoes are present, feel free to add whatever other veggies you have on hand to bulk up the dish.

FOR THE SALAD

2	tomatoes
1	cucumber
1	red onion
	parsley to taste
	feta cheese

FOR THE DRESSING

2 T	extra virgin olive oil
½ t	kosher salt
2 T	white wine vinegar
¼ t	black pepper

FOR THE SALAD

1. Slice tomatoes, cucumbers, onions and parsley. Add to large mixing bowl.
2. In a smaller bowl, combine all dressing ingredients and mix well.
3. Drizzle dressing over salad and serve topped with feta cheese crumbles.

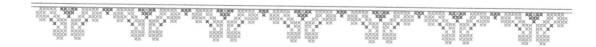

MÂNCARE DE SPANAC {spinach}

SERVES 4

Packing a nutritional punch, not all cooked spinach has to be creamed. A quick and easy side dish flavored with the smoky-salty goodness bacon has to offer.

4 lbs	fresh spinach
8 oz	bacon
1 Tbs	extra virgin olive oil
1	white onion
2-3	garlic cloves
3 T	tomato paste
	salt to taste
	pepper to taste

1. Bring a large pot of water to a boil. Add spinach to the pot in batches, allowing the spinach to wilt before crowding it with more. Cook for approximately 10 minutes.
2. Drain spinach and add to a large bowl. Set aside.
3. Cut bacon into bite-sized pieces.
4. In a frying pan, heat oil and cook bacon for approximately 2 minutes.
5. Add diced onion and quartered garlic cloves to the pan and continue cooking until onions become tender and translucent.
6. Stir in tomato paste and mix well.
7. Lower the heat and add the spinach to the pan, mixing all ingredients together. Season with salt and pepper to taste.
8. Serve warm.

MÂNCARE FOR THOUGHT . . .

Add a fried egg to the top of your spinach dish turning this recipe into a rich and velvety meal or breakfast dish.

MÂNCARE DE DOVLEAC CU MĂRAR ȘI SMÂNTÂNĂ {zucchini with dill and cream}

SERVES 4

This is the recipe, the cornerstone of From Dill To Dracula. *Whenever I think of defining Romanian recipes,* mâncare de dovleac cu mărar și smântânâ, *the literal translation of which is "pumpkin food," comes to mind. A name that better represents this recipe would be zucchini with dill and cream. As my father would say growing up, "There's no such thing as too much dill," and this recipe is proof of that. Because zucchini mimics the flavors added to it, the measurements of everything else—but the dill—are small, and yet the flavor is unlike anything you've had before. Unless, of course, this isn't your first rendezvous with this decadent recipe.*

1 ½ lbs	zucchini
½ t	kosher salt
2 T	unsalted butter
½ c	yellow onion
1 T	corn starch
2 T	heavy cream
4 T	white wine vinegar
2 T	sour cream
3 T	dill
	salt to taste
	pepper to taste

1. Using the largest holes on a grater, grate zucchini into a colander. Set in the sink to drain sprinkled with salt, covered with a paper towel and use another, heavier bowl to press the water out of the zucchini.

2. In a large pan, melt the butter and sauté the chopped onions until they become translucent. Add corn starch and heavy cream, cooking until it thickens.

3. Add in grated zucchini and continue cooking, making sure to constantly stir until the zucchini no longer gives off excess liquid.

4. Stir in white wine vinegar, sour cream, and salt and pepper to taste. Stir in dill just before serving.

MÂNCARE FOR THOUGHT . . .

Mâncare de dovleac cu mărar și smântânâ is great served immediately after cooking, when it's warm and creamy, but it also makes for great leftovers, eaten directly from the fridge!

SALATĂ DE VINETE {roasted eggplant dip}

SERVES 6

Growing up, eggplant was one of my favorite vegetables. And this recipe is no exception, embodying all the smoky goodness of an eggplant that's been charred beyond recognition, and forget the spongy eggplant texture you might be familiar with, and say hello to a creamy dollop of heaven. The only problem I ever had with it was having to wait for it to chill in the refrigerator for an hour after my mother finished preparing it. Talk about torture!

1	large eggplant
⅓ c	extra virgin olive oil
1	lemon
1	head of garlic
1-2 T	mayonnaise (optional)
	salt to taste
	pepper to taste

1. Using a fork, poke holes all around your eggplant. Get all your life frustrations out on this eggplant. Prick it all over.

2. Char the eggplant until it's black, bruised, and burned. Your method is entirely up to you (smoker, oven, etc...). I prefer to do it over a medium flame grill, to make sure it's infused with all that super smoky goodness. Don't worry about burning your eggplant; since the skin isn't used in this recipe, we want it as black as possible. The more burned, the smokier, the better.

3. Allow eggplant to cool, cut off the stem, and then cut in half length-wise. Scoop the insides out into a plastic colander, and strain the juices out by placing a paper towel over the eggplant, and pressing another bowl into the colander. A few good presses should squeeze enough of the liquid out.

4. Move the eggplant to food processor and give it a few pulses. Then add in the olive oil, juice of half a lemon, and diced garlic (or 1 yellow onion, if you prefer) until well-combined. Continue pulsing until your desired consistency.

5. Add in salt, pepper and juice of the remaining half lemon to taste.

6. If you prefer a creamier spread, mix in 1 to 2 tablespoons of mayonnaise.

7. Refrigerate for about an hour, and serve chilled or room temperature, with a good crusty bread, veggie sticks, or by spooning directly into your mouth, as I tend to do!

NOTE

Try to use plastic/wooden tools when at all possible. Metal causes the eggplant to oxidize, so you won't want it sitting in a metal colander, for instance. Using a metal knife and spoon to scoop it out quickly is one thing, but ideally any further mixing/storage would be done with wooden, plastic or glass tools.

ZACUSCĂ {roasted red pepper spread}

MAKES ONE 16OZ. JAR

Fall is the perfect time to make this recipe. With the Autumn harvest, there's an abundance of fresh vegetables with robust flavors just waiting to be made into something anew. Zacusca is smoky, salty, a little sweet, a little acidic, and fits perfectly atop a slice of crusty baguette.

1	large eggplant
2	red bell peppers
1	yellow onion
1 c	tomatoes
¼ c	vegetable oil
1	bay leaf
1 t	honey (optional)
1½ c	water
20	peppercorns
	salt to taste

1. Poke the eggplant and peppers generously with a fork and then grill the eggplant until it's charred on the outside and soft on the inside, and the red peppers until the skin is charred and blistered.
2. Alternatively, if it's too cold to grill, you can bake these on a cooking sheet in the oven at 400°F for about 20 to 30 minutes. Turn them so they can cook evenly, and make sure they're soft before removing from oven.
3. Transfer eggplant and peppers to a gallon plastic bag and allow to cool while sealed. This will make the skin removal much easier.
4. Place the skinless eggplant and peppers into a colander. Sprinkle generously with sea salt, cover with a few layers of paper towel, and set a heavier dish or bowl on top to drain as much liquid as you can from the veggies. This might take up to an hour to complete.
5. While draining the eggplant and red pepper, dice the onion and sauté in a deep pan with the oil until they become translucent. Add in the diced tomatoes.
6. Coarsely chop the eggplant and red pepper then add to the pan with your bay leaf, honey, peppercorns and water.
7. Cook on low and uncovered for about 1½ hours, stirring occasionally.
8. Adjust the taste with salt and honey if necessary.
9. Remove and discard the bay leaf, transfer contents into a food processor or blender and pulse until pureed with chunks remaining. It shouldn't be perfectly smooth.
10. Store in the fridge in an airtight container. Canning jars come in handy, though Tupperware will work, too.
11. Serve with bread, crackers or chips!

FASOLE BĂTUTĂ CU CEAPĂ CĂLITĂ {white bean dip with caramelized onion}

MAKES ABOUT 2 CUPS

There's never a shortage of garlic in Romanian recipes, and this white bean dip is no exception. A super garlicky hummus, mixed with fragrant and caramelized onions. If you're Dracula, or one of his minions, you might have to stay away from this one . . .

1 can	cannellini beans
1	carrot spear
2	bay leaves
4	garlic cloves
1 T	extra virgin olive oil
2	yellow onions
3 T	vegetable oil
	salt to taste
	pepper to taste

1. Drain and rinse beans.
2. Bring a pot of water to a boil and cook beans for approximately 20 minutes with the diced carrot, bay leaves, and seasoned with salt and pepper.
3. Before draining the beans, reserve approximately 3 tablespoons of the liquid in a small bowl.
4. Remove and discard the bay leaves.
5. Add drained beans and veggies to a food processor with the garlic, olive oil, cooked bean liquid and a touch more salt and pepper. Pulse until mixture is desired consistency, smooth and creamy, or rustic and chunky.
6. In a small frying pan, sauté diced onion in the vegetable oil over medium heat.
7. Mix onions into your bean mixture.
8. Dip can be served right away and warm, or refrigerated and cold at a later time.

MÂNCARE FOR THOUGHT . . .

Any other white bean can be used in this recipe, including a white kidney bean or chickpeas.

SOS DE CIUPERCI {mushroom dip}

MAKES ABOUT 5 CUPS

Don't you just love family recipes that omit ingredient quantities? It seems that's how a majority of traditional Romanian recipes come to exist, but with a little experimentation (and a lot of mushrooms) you can stumble upon a hearty mushroom dip like this, otherwise known as the perfect bread topper!

4 c	portabella mushrooms
1	yellow onion
1 T	vegetable oil
1 c	sour cream
1 T	mayonnaise
	fresh parsley
	green onions

1. Chop mushrooms and onion, then add to a hot saucepan with oil to sauté until onions become translucent.
2. Remove from heat and let cool completely.
3. Add sour cream and mayonnaise. Mix well.
4. Top with fresh parsley or green onions—or both!
5. Enjoy served on a slice of crusty bread.

CONOPIDĂ CU BRÂNZĂ *{cauliflower casserole with cheese}*

SERVES 6

Loaded with cheese, bacon and — of course — sour cream, this casserole is hearty and healthy, replacing the typical potato with cauliflower.

1	small cauliflower
6	bacon slices
1	yellow onion
4	garlic cloves
2	eggs
1 c	sour cream
1 c	Gruyère cheese
1 c	cheddar cheese
1 - 2 t	Hungarian paprika
	salt to taste
	pepper to taste

1. Preheat oven to 375°F.
2. Cut the cauliflower florets from the head and steam for approximately 6 minutes, or until tender.
3. In a pan, fry bacon slices. After cooking, set aside on a plate covered in paper towels to absorb some of the excess grease, but leave whatever grease remains in the pan, in the pan.
4. In the same pan you used to fry the bacon, cook the chopped onion and garlic until the onions become translucent.
5. Add steamed cauliflower to a small casserole dish. Top with crumbled bacon and your onion and garlic mixture.
6. In a small bowl, mix together eggs, sour cream, grated Gruyère and cheddar cheese, salt, pepper and paprika. Pour over the top of the casserole.
7. Bake for 25 minutes. Casserole should be bubbling and the edges should begin to brown.
8. Enjoy immediately.

ACCORDING TO FOLKLORE . . .

Conopidă de conopidă cu brânză comes from the Transylvanian region of Romanian, where none other than the (in)famous Vlad Tepes reigned. Though it's uncertain whether or not this dish would make an appearance on his dinner table, as cabbage and livestock were the more prized ingredients of that time. (And, you know, that whole garlic issue — if you believe the folklore . . .)

CARTOFI ȚĂRĂNEȘTI *{peasant potatoes}*

SERVES 4

Whether you call them peasant potatoes or home fries, crispy bits of fried potato are the perfect side to a hearty, meaty meal—or as a standalone dish to enjoy year-round!

2 lbs	redskin potatoes
3 T	extra virgin olive oil
2	white onions
⅛ t	salt
1 T	Hungranian paprika
	pepper to taste
	fresh dill to taste

1. Peel your potatoes and dice them into bite-sized pieces.
2. Heat oil over a medium flame. Add chopped onion and a dash of salt, cooking until onions become translucent.
3. Add in your potatoes, salt and pepper to taste. Cook until the potatoes soften and crisp.
4. Finish with paprika and cook for 1 more minute, making sure it doesn't burn.
5. Sprinkled chopped dill and serve immediately.

CARTOFI ROTUNZI
CU OUĂ FIERTE TARI {scalloped potatoes with hard boiled eggs}

SERVES 4

Cheesy, eggy and potato-y . . . the definition of comfort food. A Romanian twist on the French Au Gratin Potatoes, the addition of hard boiled eggs and sour cream mix to compliment each other in a warm and hearty bite.

6	russet potatoes
8	eggs
½ c	unsalted butter
1 c	sour cream
1 c	shredded cheddar cheese
	salt to taste
	pepper to taste

1. Wash the skin of the potato and boil them in salted water until it can be pricked easily with a fork.
2. At the same time, hard boil the eggs by adding eggs to a pot of water, and allow to reach a boil. Once boiling, remove eggs from heat, cover, and let sit for 8 minutes. After time has passed, drain pot and rinse with cold water to halt cooking.
3. Preheat oven to 400°F.
4. Peel skin off of potatoes, and remove eggs from their shell. Slice both into medallions.
5. Butter a glass or ceramic baking dish.
6. Begin with a layer of potatoes, and then a layer of eggs, salting and peppering each layer before you add to it. You should end up with two layers of potatoes, and two layers of eggs, ending with eggs on top.
7. Pour sour cream over top.
8. Cook for 30 minutes. Remove from oven and top with shredded cheddar cheese.
9. Reduce oven to 350°F and continue cooking for 15 minutes, or until cheese has melted.
10. Remove from oven and allow potatoes to cool for approximately 15 minutes before serving.

SALATĂ DE CARTOFI *{potato salad}*

SERVES 4

This is it. No need to look any further. You've found the perfect cold potato salad for a summer picnic!

2 lb	white potatoes
¾ t	kosher salt
¼ t	black pepper
½ c	white onion
3 T	white vinegar
¼ c	vegetable oil
2 T	fresh chives

1. Bring a large pot of water to boil and add in whole, skin-on potatoes. Cook for approximately 25 minutes, or until soft enough to prick with a fork. Remove from the pot and allow to slightly cool in a single layer on a flat surface.
2. When potatoes are cool enough to touch, but still warm, carefully peel off the skin.
3. Slice into thin medallions and add to a medium-sized bowl. Season with salt and pepper. Stir in diced onions and white vinegar, mixing to combine.
4. Add vegetable oil and mix to combine.
5. Serve chilled and topped with fresh chives.

SALATĂ DE CASTRAVEȚI {cucumber salad}

SERVES 4

I promise you'll drool over this super simple summer salad as much as I'm drooling over that alliteration. The tang of vinegar coats the crisp freshness of cucumbers, leaving you with a burst of bright flavors.

2	cucumbers
1	yellow onion
½ T	kosher salt
⅓ c	white vinegar
1 t	extra virgin olive oil
	fresh dill to taste

1. Wash and peel cucumber, then slice into thin medallions and add to a medium bowl.
2. Add sliced onion and season with salt. Mix to combine.
3. Set aside to marinate for 20 minutes.
4. Drain the excess water from the bottom of the bowl after the time has passed. Add vinegar and extra virgin olive oil. Mix to combine.
5. Serve chilled and topped with fresh dill.

MĂMĂLIGĂ {corn porridge}

SERVES 6 BOWLS

Nothing is more homey than a warm bowl of corn porridge covered in salty bacon and sour cheese. Mămăligă is a quick meal you can whip up any day of the week and get creative with the toppings added to it, from sausage to . . . you guessed it: sour cream!

8 c	water
1 t	kosher salt
2 c	cornmeal
	bacon
	feta cheese

1. Bring salted water to a boil. Reduce heat and slowly whisk in cornmeal, stirring continuously to keep from clumping. Cornmeal will thicken as it cooks.
2. As cornmeal cooks, preheat oven and cook bacon slices according to its package. A little crispier than normal is better.
3. Continue cooking and stirring cornmeal for 20 to 30 minutes.
4. To serve, spoon cornmeal into a bowl and top with a healthy helping of crumbled bacon and feta cheese.

MÂNCARE FOR THOUGHT . . .

Mămăligă is often considered the national food of Romania. It used to be considered "poor man's bread" as it was more common than finding bread on your dinner plate.

BULZ *{stuffed grilled polenta}*

MAKES 5

A variation of the beloved Mămăligă, stuffed with your favorite salty ingredients. Think of it as a Romanian Hot Pocket that'll melt in your mouth and energize your tastebuds. You'll find Bulz being cooked on the street by local vendors, grilled to perfection and oozing with delicious melted cheese.

8 c	water
1 t	kosher salt
2 c	cornmeal

OPTIONAL FILLINGS

sheep cheese

ham

bacon

1. Bring salted water to a boil. Reduce heat and slowly whisk in cornmeal, stirring continuously to keep from clumping. Cornmeal will thicken as it cooks.
2. As cornmeal cooks, preheat oven and cook bacon slices according to its package. A little crispier than normal is better.
3. Continue cooking and stirring cornmeal for 20 to 30 minutes.
4. Pour cornmeal into another bowl and allow to cool.
5. Once cooled, take a fistful of cornmeal and shape it into a ball about the size of a medium apple.
6. Fill cornmeal ball with your favorite ingredients, such as fresh sheep cheese and ham.
7. Close your cornmeal ball so that all the inside ingredients are enclosed.
8. Grill on an open flame until the outside becomes crispy.
9. Serve topped with sour cream or a perfectly fried egg.

MÂNCARE FOR THOUGHT . . .

Bulz *are also known as* Urs de Mămăligă *(polenta bear) or* Gasca de Mămăligă *(goose polenta).*

VARZĂ CĂLITĂ {braised cabbage}

SERVES 6

Cabbage is a popular vegetable in the Transylvania region of Romania. The perfect recipe for a cold winter, this braised cabbage recipe is so surprisingly jam-packed with flavor. It can feature as it's own dish, or as a popular side dish to your favorite protein alongside Mămăligă, another Romanian favorite. While it's not a dip or spread, per se, it is a great addition to a crusty bread.

2	bell peppers
2	white onions
2	medium tomatoes
2 t	smoked garlic powder
1	cabbage
3 T	tomato paste
3	smoked sausages
1	bay leaf
	extra virgin olive oil
	salt to taste
	pepper to taste

1. Cook the chopped peppers and onions in oil over low heat until the onions become translucent. Add in chopped tomatoes and season with salt and pepper to taste, and smoked garlic powder. Cook for 2 to 3 minutes.

2. While vegetables are cooking, wash and chop the cabbage into thin strips, similar to a sauerkraut.

3. Add tomato paste and chopped smoked sausage (can sub for ground Italian sausage) and bay leaf to your pan of vegetables. Cover and let simmer for a few minutes.

4. Add your cabbage to the pan and continue cooking uncovered. The cabbage may not fit all at once. Add to the pan in batches if this is the case.

5. Let cabbage simmer on low heat for approximately 10 minutes, stirring frequently. Then, cover and let cook for an additional 10 minutes.

6. Season with salt and pepper, remove the bay leaf and enjoy warm.

RASNOV, ROMANIA

CARNE

{meat}

MICI *{grilled sausages}*

MAKES 12-16 SAUSAGES

A summer picnic staple grilled over an open flame, Mici are tender, juicy sausages that aren't unlike hamburger, and eaten on bread like a hot dog, or by itself and dipped in a yellow mustard. Nothing says summer like grilling, and Mici make for the best grilling foods during a Romanian summer.

3	garlic cloves
1 lb	ground pork
1 lb	ground beef
2 t	baking soda
2 T	extra virgin olive oil
½ t	hot paprika
½ t	dried thyme
2 t	caraway seeds
1 t	black pepper
½ t	red pepper flakes
2 t	kosher salt

1. Mince garlic until fine.
2. In a large bowl, use your hands to mix all ingredients together, frequently wetting your hands while mixing will help keep the mixture moist.
3. Form into small 3" long sausages, approximately ¾" thick. Cut the edges off to form little cylinders.
4. Place sausages in the refrigerator for a couple of hours to allow the meat to set. This will make them juicy and tender.
5. Grill on a hot grill until cooked through, turning with tongs approximately every 4 minutes. Don't pierce with a fork while cooking.
6. Serve dipped in yellow mustard with a side of crusty bread.

LET'S LEARN ROMANIAN . . .

Depending on where you are in Romania, Mici (pronounced mm-each) might be called Mititei (pronounced me-tea-tay). Regardless of their name, they're just as delicious.

CHIFTELE *{meatballs}*

SERVES 6

Meatballs are an ancient culinary tradition. Almost every culture has their own variation of the dish, which appears to have begun in Northern India, according to early records. Chiftele are very similar to the Middle Eastern Keftas, a key distinction in that the Romanian variation uses fresh vegetables mixed with the meat, and has them fried in oil. They're hearty and delicious, the perfect addition to a meat-lacking meal, or perfect just the way they are.

1	white bread slice
1 lb	ground pork
1 lb	ground lamb
1	white onion
1	russet potato
2	garlic cloves
½	sprig of dill
½	sprig of parsley
1	celery stalk
1	carrot spear
½ t	kosher salt
½ t	black pepper
¼ t	nutmeg
3 T	cold water
2	eggs
	all-purpose flour
	vegetable oil

1. Soak a slice of white bread in water.
2. Add both ground meats, onion, peeled potato, garlic, half a sprig of fresh dill and parsley, celery, carrot and salt and pepper to a food processor. Pulse until finely chopped. Then sprinkle in nutmeg.
3. Transfer to a large bowl and mix with the soaked slice of bread, cold water, and eggs. Mix using your hands until well-combined.
4. Set aside in the refrigerator for 30 minutes.
5. Form 1" meatballs by hand and roll in a light dusting of flour.
6. Heat vegetable oil in a large frying pan over medium heat. Gently add meatballs and cook for approximately 1 minute per side, or until cooked through.
7. Remove from oil and transfer to a plate lined in paper towel.

MÂNCARE FOR THOUGHT . . .

Add Chiftele to your favorite soup broth, stew in a tomato sauce, or pop 'em in your mouth by themselves—they're delicious on their own, too!

FEATURED FOOD

SLANINA {smoked bacon}

As is with many smoked Romanian meats, *salanina* is a pork product made from the abdominal area or the back of a pig, and tends to be more fat than meat. It's cured and smoked, and then ready to eat! Or, if you're like me, you stock up on your pieces of *salanina* so you never run out. Since it's cured, it can be stored in your refrigerator or freezer for quite a while. It can be used as a bacon replacement in recipes, or to give your morning eggs a smoky, meaty flavor.

Salanina sparkles over a Summer bonfire. I have the best memories of sitting around a flickering and popping bonfire, fireflies and stars overhead, and good company all around, with a hefty cutting of *salanina* roasting over the fire. Sure, the meat itself is delicious after its been licked by the flames, but what we're really looking for is the drippings. While the *salanina* is heating, you'd hold a piece of crusty, homemade bread (like my *Tară Pâine* on page 45) just below to catch all the fatty drippings before they could escape into the flames.

That's really the best part.
That's the definition of Summer.

POMANA PORCULUI *{roasted pork}*

SERVES 4 TO 6

These crispy little pork poppers are a quick and easy meal or side dish.

2 lb	pork tenderloin
2 T	vegetable oil
1 c	white wine
	salt to taste
	pepper to taste
	dried thyme to taste

1. Dice pork tenderloin into bite-sized pieces.
2. Heat the oil in a large frying pan. Add pork and cook through.
3. When finished cooking, douse with wine and season to taste with spices and herbs to personal taste.

FEATURED FOOD

PIFTIE *{pork jelly}*

Also known as *Răcitură* in the northern cities. *Piftie* is a popular dish you'll find on a Christmas table, and a trademark recipe of Romania. It's a hardy meal that pairs perfectly with another Romanian staple: *Mămăligă* (page 111).

Before you fly by this page at the sight of those two words together, give pork jelly a chance! Yes, *Piftie* is typically made from pig feet that have been jellied into an aspic, but it's also such a uniquely Romanian dish that's very much unlike anything else.

The process of preparation is fairly simple, though what takes the most time is in waiting for the gelatin to set. The chunks of pork are boiled with carrots, garlic and parsley and then allowed to congeal in the fridge until a natural jelly is formed. When eaten, it's dusted with a heavy-hand of paprika. Some people eat the pork with the jelly. Others eat just the pork. And then there's those in my camp, who only have eyes on the jelly.

Either way you prefer to eat it, if you're able to get your hands on this aspic it's worth a taste. Who knows, you might fall in love with something you never thought you would.

CLĂTITE CU CARNE {pancake with meat}

MAKES 7 PANCAKES

This recipe features a light and thin pancake wrapped around minced meat and mushrooms, a great on-the-go bite, or as a meal and topped with a mushroom cream sauce.

FOR THE PANCAKE

2	eggs
⅛ t	salt
1¼ c	milk
3 T	unsalted butter
1 c	all-purpose four
2 T	sparkling water

FOR THE FILLING

1 T	extra virgin olive oil
½ lb	ground pork
1	garlic clove
1	white onion
1	celery stick
1	small bell pepper
2 c	white mushrooms
7 T	dry white wine
1	egg yolk
5½ T	heavy cream
1½ T	unsalted butter
	parsley to taste
	salt to taste
	pepper to taste

FOR THE SAUCE (OPTIONAL)

1 T	extra virgin olive oil
1 T	unsalted butter
1	shallot
1¼ c	white mushrooms
¾ c	heavy cream
1 t	corn starch
	parsley to taste
	salt to taste
	pepper to taste

FOR THE PANCAKE

1. Whisk eggs in a bowl with salt, milk and melted butter.
2. Gradually add flour in tablespoon increments until fully combined and smooth.
3. Stir in mineral water (alternatively, flat water will work as well) until combined. You should end up with a thin batter consistency. If you allow batter to sit for too long it will thicken. A little additional milk or water will bring it back to the desired consistency.
4. Spray a shallow, non-stick frying pan with cooking spray and heat on the stove.
5. Pour a ladle of batter in the center of the pan, and in a circular motion, rotate the pan until the batter has spread to its edges and forms a thin pancake.
6. Pancake is ready to be flipped with the top is no longer glossy and the edges start to curl. Watch carefully, as the pancake is thin and cooks quickly, no more than 1 to 2 minutes.
7. After both sides have cooked, remove from heat and set aside on a large plate. Begin preparing the filling and sauce.

FOR THE FILLING

1. Heat oil in a pan and cook ground pork until it's no longer pink. Transfer to a plate and set aside.
2. In the same pan, add finely diced onion, celery, bell pepper and mushrooms. Season with salt and cook until vegetables are tender.
3. Add the cooked ground pork back to the pan and deglaze with wine. Cook until most of the wine has evaporated. Season again with salt and pepper to taste. Transfer to a bowl and allow to cool.
4. Once cooled, mix in egg yolk and chopped parsley (to taste) until fully combined.
5. Preheat oven to 375°F.

CLĂTITE CU CARNE *continued...*

6. Grease a baking dish and set aside.
7. To assemble the meat pancake, add approximately 2 tablespoons of meat mixture in a line, slightly off-center on one pancake. Fold the short edge over the mixture, length-wise. Like rolling a burrito, seal the edges by folding them over the two ends of the line of meat. Finish by rolling until the remainder of the pancake has been folded over. Repeat until all pancakes have been used. See note for a step-by-step diagram.
8. Line meat pancakes in a row in your baking dish.
9. Pour heavy cream and cubed butter over the meat pancakes.
10. Cook in oven for 20 to 25 minutes. Prepare the optional sauce while you wait.

FOR THE SAUCE (OPTIONAL)

1. Heat oil in a small saucepan. Add butter and finely chopped shallots. Cook until translucent.
2. Add finely chopped mushrooms. Cook for an additional 3 to 4 minutes.
3. Stir in heavy cream and corn starch, mixing until combined.
4. Remove from heat, and add chopped parsley. Season with salt and pepper to taste.

FOR THE SERVING

1. Remove baking dish from the oven and allow to cool for 10 minutes.
2. Serve topped with mushroom cream sauce, or your favorite dipping sauce of choice.

NOTE

Here's a helpful diagram showing step-by-step how the pancake should be filled and rolled.

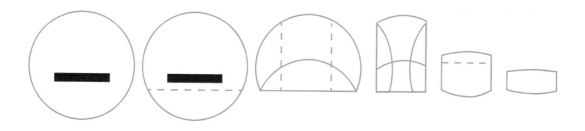

FEATURED FOOD

JUMĂRI *{pork graves}*

Jumări is a true treat in my household, little golden nuggets of pork fat, fried in more fat, and sprinkled with salt.

You could say they're the Romanian equivalent to pork graves, though *Jumări* pieces vary between just fat and fat with a little bit of meat (those are always my favorite). Most pieces don't have as much of a crunch, which is why they easily melt once you take a bite. It's really a delicacy.

The only downside I've ever been able to find when it comes to *Jumări* is how it's self-monitoring in the quantity you're able to consume. Because of the nature of *Jumări*, it's an incredibly greasy delicacy, and eating too much can cause an upset stomach. That's why it's always recommended to eat with a nice crusty bread, like my *Tară Pâine* (page 45).

ȘNIȚEL DE PUI *{egg chicken}*

SERVES 2

Egg chicken—or eggy chicken, if you grew up in my family—is a Romanian take on the ever-popular German Schnitzel, but features chicken breast opposed to the traditional pork. The light crackling as the egg fries up around the thinly sliced chicken will be music to your ears, and a signal to your stomach that it's almost time to enjoy!

2	skinless chicken breast
1 c	all-purpose flour
2 t	salt
1 t	black pepper
2	eggs
1 c	very fine breadcrumbs
	vegetable oil

1. Place the chicken breast between two pieces of plastic wrap and, using a meat tenderizer, rolling pin, or thick cooking book (just not this one) to hammer the chicken until it becomes a thin breast, a little less than ¼" thickness. Repeat with the second breast.

2. Prepare three shallow dishes, filling one with the flour, salt and pepper, the second with the beaten eggs, and the third with the breadcrumbs.

3. Dredge one chicken breast through the flour, shaking off any excess. Then dip into the beaten eggs, allowing the excess to drip back into the bowl. Finally, pass the chicken breast through the breadcrumbs, making sure it's well-coated. Repeat for the second breast.

4. Heat vegetable oil in a frying pan. Once hot, add both to the pan and cook for approximately 3 to 5 minutes on each side.

5. Serve with your favorite side dish!

NOTE

If you're unable to find very fine breadcrumbs, you can create your own by adding your breadcrumbs to a plastic bag and rolling over it with a rolling pin, or pulsing a few times in a food processor.

CIULAMA DE PUI {creamed chicken}

SERVES 8 BOWLS

Similar to a chicken fricassee, this creamy chicken dish is the definition of comfort food, and causes families to flock to the kitchen table, ready to loosen their belts and fill their plates. Simple and delicious, yet packed with decadent flavor, make sure you grab your favorite part of the chicken (no doubt the drumstick) before someone else takes it away!

1	yellow onion
4	garlic cloves
3	celery stalks
2	carrot spears
1	whole chicken
3	add'l drumsticks
3	add'l thighs
1 lb	cremini mushrooms
2 T	all-purpose flour
2 c	heavy cream
1 T	Hungarian paprika
	salt to taste
	pepper to taste
	fresh dill to taste

1. Preheat oven to 325°F.
2. Dice onions, garlic, celery, and carrots, and mix together in a large bowl.
3. Divide the vegetable mixture, placing half in a baking dish. Top with a layer of broken-down chicken, and then top the chicken with the remaining vegetables.
4. Cover baking dish, either with a lid or aluminum foil, and bake for 1 hour.
5. While chicken cooks, heat a frying pan over medium-high heat, and cook mushrooms until they begin to wilt and they develop a brown hue. Remove from heat and set aside.
6. Check the chicken and vegetables. If the chicken looks undercooked (if you have a meat thermometer, the internal temperature should be 165°) then continue cooking covered for 20 minute intervals. If the chicken is cooked through, remove from oven.
7. In a small bowl, whisk flour and cream together until smooth. Add cream, paprika and mushrooms to your chicken and vegetables, re-cover dish and continue baking for 30 minutes.
8. Remove from the oven and stir all the ingredients together. Season with salt, pepper and fresh chopped dill to taste.

FEATURED FOOD

CÂRNAȚI {pork dry sausage}

It wouldn't be summer at my grandparent's house until ropes of sausage hung from the rafters of their garage, and the dense, deep smokiness emanated through the entire house. My grandfather made the best *Cârnați*, and waiting for it to dry in the garage was always a test of patience.

This dry pork sausage, a mix of pork, beef and poultry, is jam-packed with paprika and garlic and, as I've mentioned before, the more the better when it comes to Romanian cooking. *Cârnați* can be eaten fried or, my own personal favorite, just as it is—no strings attached.

The best sausages can't be purchased from a store. They're made in a home, with a lot of love, a lot of garlic and a lot of paprika.

SARMALE *{cabbage rolls}*

SERVES 6

1	head of cabbage
1	yellow onion
2	garlic cloves
2½ T	white rice
3½ c	water
1	white bread slice
2 lbs	ground pork
6 oz	bacon
2 T	fresh dill
1 t	ground thyme
2 t	kosher salt
1 t	black pepper
1 t	red pepper flakes
1 c	sauerkraut juice
1 T	Vegeta®
10	peppercorns
4	bay leaves
3 c	sauerkraut
2 lbs	tomatoes
	extra virgin olive oil

1. Remove outer green leaves from the cabbage and set aside. Cut out the core of the cabbage and clean. Blanch the pulled apart leaves for approximately 2 minutes, and the cored cabbage for approximately 1 minute. Do not use these outer leaves to assemble the rolls.

2. With two forks, gently peel off as many leaves as you're able. Repeat blanching the cabbage until all or most leaves have been removed.

3. Heat olive oil in a pan over medium-high heat and cook diced onion, minced garlic and raw rice until the onions become translucent and the rice browns.

4. Lower heat and add ¼ cup of water to the pan. Simmer for approximately 10 minutes, or until the rice has absorbed all the liquid. Set aside to cool.

5. Soak the slice of bread in water and squeeze out the excess. Add to a bowl with ground pork, and onion and rice mixture. Stir to combine.

6. Add dill, thyme, salt, pepper, red pepper flakes, and 2 tablespoons of water to the bowl. Mix until combined.

7. In a separate bowl, mix 3 cups of water, sauerkraut juice, Vegeta®, peppercorns and bay leaves together.

8. Squeeze as much water as you're able from the sauerkraut using a towel or sieve.

9. Prepare a Dutch oven with 2 tablespoons of olive oil, a layer of sauerkraut, and then a layer of bacon strips.

10. To assemble, take one cabbage leaf in the palm of your hand. Add a small amount of the meat mixture to the center of the leaf and shape to form a little sausage near the base of the leaf. Wrap by covering one side of the leaf over the meat, and then the other.

11. Repeat process until all cabbage leaves and mixture has been used, placing each cabbage roll tightly together in the bottom of your Dutch oven. Add any remaining sauerkraut or cabbage scraps to the Dutch oven, drizzle with olive oil, and pour the sauerkraut and water mixture over top. Cover the tops of the cabbage rolls with the outer leaves you had set aside to keep the moisture in.

12. Preheat oven to 375°F.

13. Cook Dutch oven over high heat until the sauce begins to bubble. Lower to medium-low heat, cover and continue simmering for 20 minutes.

14. Continue cooking covered in the oven for 1½ hours. Then add sliced tomatoes to the pot and continue cooking for an additional hour, removing the lid for the final 15 minutes of cooking. Don't worry — there's no overcooking these cabbage rolls!

15. Serve hot and with a generous dollop of sour cream!

VARZĂ À LA CLUJ *{deconstructed cabbage rolls}*

SERVES 6

Looking for an easier alternative to Sarmale? Look no further than Varza à la Cluj, *a deconstructed version to the tightly wrapped cabbage rolls on the previous page. All the same, comforting ingredients are mixed together in bowl-form, making it a quicker, simpler option if you're short of time, or those pesky cabbage leaves just aren't cooperating.*

1	head of cabbage
½ c	water
1	sprig of thyme
¾ c	white rice
2	sausages of choice (optional)
2	yellow onions
1 lb	ground pork
1 lb	ground beef
3 T	extra virgin olive oil
7 T	tomato paste
	salt to taste
	pepper to taste

1. Cut the cabbage into thin strips, season with salt and fry in oil. When the cabbage wilts, add water and continue to stir. Add a sprig of thyme and continue to cook until all the water evaporates.
2. While the cabbage is cooking, boil the rice according to its package directions.
3. Chop the sausages (optional) into medallions. In a separate pan, cook through, then set aside.
4. Chop the onions. In a separate pan, cook the onions until they become translucent. When they do, add the ground pork and beef, and season with salt and pepper. Continue cooking until the juice reduces.
5. Once the rice is cooked, add it to the meat and continue cooking for 5 minutes, stirring frequently.
6. Preheat your oven to 350°F.
7. Mix olive oil with tomato paste.
8. Prepare a high-rimmed baking dish with nonstick spray. Spread layers alternating between the cabbage and the meat/rice, interspersing the tomato paste mixture and chopped sausages (optional) in between the layers. It's important for the cabbage to end as the top layer.
9. Cook for 1 hour.
10. Serve warm with your favorite sides.

FEATURED FOOD

TOBĂ {head cheese}

Waste not. That's the theory behind *Tobă*, an aspic made from all the otherwise unused (but arguably the best) bits of an animal, things like the ears, snout, tail and a few of the organs. It's popular around Christmas time, but delicious all year round, especially when eaten with a strong mustard and salty pickle. The ingredients are all added to a stomach casing and become suspended in a jelly, which is left to set as a wide, sausage-like roll and cut into thick medallions.

ARDEI UMPLUȚI {stuffed bell peppers}

MAKES 4 PEPPERS

Stuffed peppers are a European staple, so there's no doubt Romania has their own take on the recipe. Similar to the previous Chiftele *recipe (page 122),* Ardei Umpluți *utilizes a slice of white bread soaked in water to add an extra depth and texture to the rice and meat. They're doused in a homemade tomato sauce that just screams* Mănâncă-mă! *{Eat me}!*

1	white bread slice
¼ c	white rice
4	bell peppers
1	yellow onion
1 lb	ground pork
1 t	kosher salt
1 t	black pepper
2 c	tomato puree
½ c	sour cream
2 c	water
	parsley to taste
	sour cream to taste

1. Soak a slice of white bread in water.
2. Cook rice according to its package.
3. Preheat oven to 400°F.
4. Prepare a large baking dish for the peppers.
5. Wash and cut the tops off the peppers. Set tops aside.
6. Remove the pepper's ribs and seeds.
7. In a large bowl, mix diced onion, ground pork, soaked slice of bread, cooked rice, ½ teaspoon of salt and ½ teaspoon of black pepper.
8. Fill peppers all the way to the top with the mixture and place upright in your baking dish.
9. In a medium bowl, begin making the sauce by mixing tomato puree, sour cream, water, ½ teaspoon of salt and ½ teaspoon of black pepper together.
10. Pour sauce over the top of the peppers.
11. Set cut-off tops of peppers back on the pepper they came from.
12. Cover peppers with aluminum foil and bake for 1½ hours.
13. Check peppers. If meat is not fully cooked, bake for another 30 minutes.
14. Serve with crusty bread, sour cream and chopped parsley.

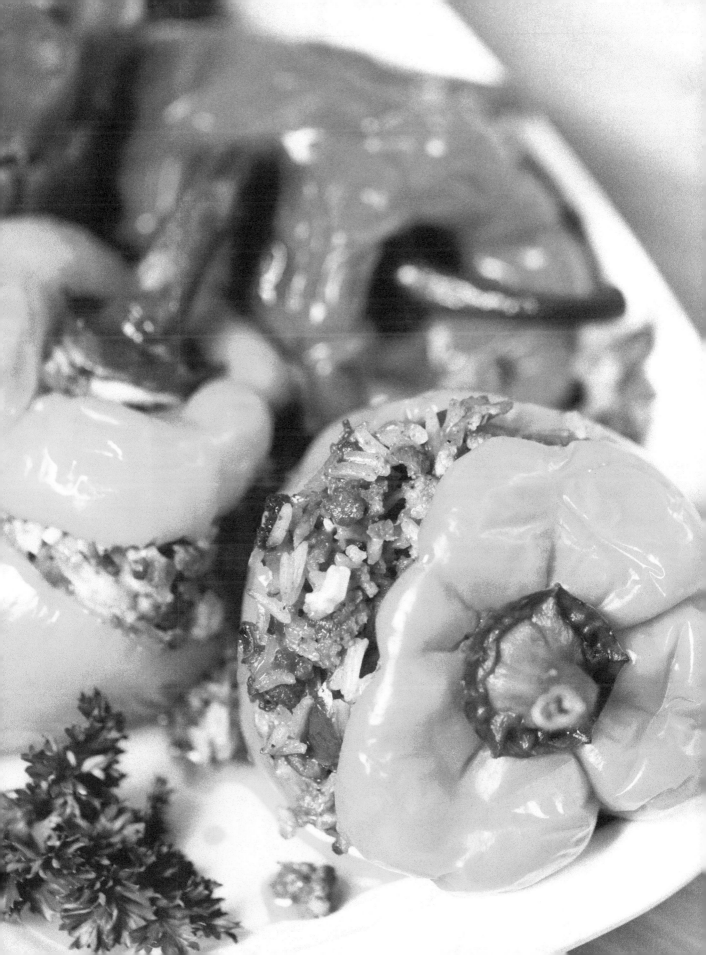

SALATĂ DE BOEUF {beef salad}

SERVES 6

This salad is the definition of versatility. Don't eat beef? Sub chicken! Don't eat meat? Omit beef! Have a lot of veggies you need to get rid of? Dice 'em up and throw 'em in! A twist on a potato salad that's perfect for your next summer picnic.

1 lb	stew beef
1 lb	russet potatoes
½ lb	carrots
½ c	frozen peas
1 c	pickles
1 c	mayonnaise
4 T	mustard
	salt to taste
	pepper to taste

1. Bring a pot of salted water to a boil and add beef, cooking until tender, approximately one hour.
2. In a second pot, bring potatoes to a boil and cook until potatoes can be pricked easily with a fork. Drain water and re-fill with cold water to halt cooking.
3. Peel carrots and, in a third pot, bring salted water to a boil and cook carrots until they're tender, approximately 25 minutes. Drain and set aside and let cool.
4. In a fourth pot, bring salted water to a boil and add peas, cooking for no more than five minutes,
5. Add cooked peas to a large bowl.
6. Peel potatoes and dice remaining vegetables (including pickles) and beef into small pieces.
7. Add mayonnaise and mustard to the diced vegetables and beef. Mix and season with salt and pepper to taste.
8. Refrigerate before serving.

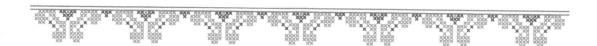

CABANA VLĂDEASA, ROMANIA

DULCIURI

{sweets}

BULGĂRE DE ZĂPADĂ {snowball cookies}

MAKES 2 - 3 DOZEN

I'm pretty sure every culture has their own version of this cookie, but I'm definitely partial to the ones my grandmother would make for Christmas, that utilize the popular Romanian ingredient: walnuts. This crumbly, nutty cookie won't hold its shape for long if you take a bite, so you pop the entire thing in your mouth!

1 c	unsalted butter
½ c	powdered sugar
1 t	vanilla extract
⅔ c	walnuts
2¼ c	all-purpose flour
¼ t	kosher salt

1. Preheat oven to 400°F.
2. In a stand mixer bowl, mix softened butter, powdered sugar and vanilla extract.
3. Using a food processor, grind the walnuts to a coarse powder. Add to the mixer bowl with the flour and salt. Mix until combined.
4. Prepare a baking tray with parchment paper, and roll dough into small 1" balls.
5. Bake for 10 minutes, or until cookies are just beginning to brown.
6. Remove from oven and transfer cookies to a wire cooling rack. Before they cool completely, but also aren't hot to the touch, roll cookies in more powdered sugar.

COZONAC CU MAC {sweet bread filled with poppy seeds}

MAKES 4 BREAD LOGS

Prepare to dream — or at the very least salivate — over this puffy bread rope with a generous, spiral-like galaxy core of creamy poppy seed filling. Even though it's typically prepared for the holidays, you'll want to make it year-round once you get a taste of the sweet poppy filling.

FOR THE DOUGH

8 c	all-purpose flour
2⅔ c	milk
1 t	active dry yeast
1 T	granulated sugar
7 T	unsalted butter
13 T	powdered sugar
8	egg yolks
⅛ t	salt
1 t	vanilla extract
	zest of lemon

FOR THE FILLING

1 can	poppy seed pie filling
1½ c	milk
⅔ c	granulated sugar
1 t	vanilla extract
1 t	ground cinnamon
	zest of lemon

FOR THE DOUGH

1. In a large mixing bowl, combine 4 cups of flour and milk. Leave on the counter at room temperature for 20 minutes. Dough should become sticky.
2. While waiting, in another bowl mix remaining half cup of flour with yeast, sugar and half a cup of milk together. Leave on the counter at room temperature for 20 minutes.
3. After 20 minutes have passed, combine the two bowls together and add the sugar, melted butter, 6 egg yokes, salt, vanilla and lemon zest.
4. Add the remaining 3½ cups of flour, and use your hands to knead the dough until it's combined and can be shaped into a ball. Cover with a clean tea towel and leave at room temperature for 40 minutes. Dough will rise.
5. During this time, prepare the filling by mixing all the ingredients together in a small saucepan, bringing it to a boil, for about 2 minutes, and stirring constantly so that the poppy seeds don't burn to the bottom of the pan. Remove from heat and let thicken.
6. After 40 minutes have passed, preheat the oven to 325°F and retrieve the dough, which should have doubled. Roll from bowl to a floured surface and divide into 4 equal sections.
7. With a rolling pin, roll each dough section out to approximately 12x8" and ½" thick.
8. Spread poppy seed filling across each rolled-out dough sheet, an inch from the edge.
9. Fold the short ends of the dough over its edge of poppy seeds, then roll the long end of the dough on itself and the filling until it's all rolled up. Repeat for each dough sheet.
10. Place rolls side-by-side on a baking sheet lined with parchment paper. Use parchment paper between the rolls to keep them from baking into one another, also.
11. In a small bowl, mix 2 egg yolks with remaining milk, and brush atop each roll, which will give the bread it's rich brown color.
12. Bake for 1 hour, checking at 50 minutes. If the bread looks like it's browning too much, cover with aluminum foil for the remaining time.
13. Allow to cool completely before removing from the baking sheet.
14. Serve cut into ½" cookies.

SALAM DE BISCUIȚI {chocolate salami roll}

MAKES 2 ROLLS

If you're looking for something quick, easy, no-bake, and that uses ingredients you likely already have stocked up in your pantry, then Salam de Biscuiti *is your recipe. I imagine that's exactly how it came to be in the Old Country: using up whatever ingredients were left over after a week, month, season. Waste not, but enjoy every bite!*

16 T	butter
1 c	granulated sugar
1½ T	water
2 T	cocoa powder
4 t	rum extract
1 lb	crackers animal

BEFORE BEGINNING THE RECIPE
Leave the butter out until it softens, about an hour.

1. In a saucepan, add the sugar, water and cocoa. Bring to a boil, then add in the rum extract. Taste the liquid to make sure the rum is strong and the syrup is very sweet.
2. In a plastic bag, or the bag the animal crackers come in, crush the crackers until all are broken but larger chunks remain. They should not be crushed to a powder.
3. In a large bowl, add the crushed animal crackers and softened sticks of butter then pour the hot syrup over it. Mix ingredients together until it becomes fudge-like. I like to use my hands for this part, just to make sure everything is even and coated. It also helps with the next step . . .
4. Prepare a sheet of plastic wrap on the counter. Shape mixture a log and roll tightly in the plastic wrap.
5. Refrigerate overnight or until the mixture is set (approximately 3 hours).
6. Store in the refrigerator, and cut into salami like slices when ready to eat!

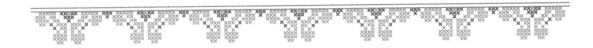

CORNULEȚE CU RAHAT {tiny horns filled with jelly}

MAKES 48 HORNS

With Romanian cuisine you'll start to grow a fond appreciation for the humble prune and its many transformations. Its strong flavor and sweet essence is the perfect filling for this flaky, unsweetened dough. Sometimes less is more, sometimes you don't need to pile on the sugar for a delightfully sweet treat. And sometimes more is more, as is the case with these Cornulețe—you can't stop at just one! (But it's okay to indulge in more because they're tiny horns, not gargantuan horns.)

2 c	all-purpose flour
½ c	sour cream
3	egg yolks
10½ T	unsalted butter
1	splash of vanilla extract
⅛ t	pinch of salt
1	jar of your favorite jam
	powdered sugar

1. Prepare a stand mixer and add flour, sour cream, egg yolks, refrigerated butter, cut into cubes, a splash of vanilla extract and salt to its bowl. Mix until fully combined, but not over mixed.

2. Form dough into a ball and wrap in plastic wrap. Refrigerate for at least 1 hour.

3. When you're ready to bake, preheat oven to 350°F.

4. Remove dough from refrigerator and let it sit out on your counter for 30 minutes to reach room temperature.

5. On a floured surface, divide dough into four equal parts. Working with one, roll until it's about 10 to 12" in diameter. Dough should be thin.

6. Using a pizza roller or butter knife, cut out 12 triangular slices from the dough. Think of it like you're cutting a pizza.

7. Use a small spoon to transfer a small dollop of jam to the wide end of the triangle. Prune or apricot jams are traditional, however you can sub with whatever you prefer or have on hand.

8. Roll the wide end of the triangle over on itself, and continue rolling until the tail curls over itself, like a croissant.

9. Repeat steps 5 through 8 until all four dough balls have been used.

10. Place in even rows on a parchment paper lined baking sheet

11. Bake for 20 minutes, checking at 15 minutes. You'll want to pull them out just as they begin to brown. If your horns are smaller, baking time will be shorter, and vise versa if they're larger.

12. Dust with powdered sugar immediately after pulling out of the oven. Since the dough does not contain its own sugar, this is an important step.

NAPOLITANE CU CARAMEL ŞI NUCI {wafer with caramel and nuts}

MAKES ONE 9X12" CAKE

This cookie, belonged to me as a kid—each of the grandchildren had their own recipe, and Napolitane Cu Cacao Si Nuci was all mine. I have the fondest of memories breaking apart the wafers from one another and licking the nutty cream from each layer. You could consider them the Oreo® of Romania. (I'd even argue these are better!)

1 c	walnuts
2 T	all-purpose flour
1 c	milk
1½ c	granulated sugar
10 t	water
7 T	unsalted butter
1 T	rum extract
4	wafer sheets

1. Place walnuts in a plastic bag and crush with either a rolling pin, or by pulsing a few times in a food processor. They should be crushed to a fine powder.
2. In a small bowl, whisk the flour and milk together until smooth, making sure no lumps of flour remain.
3. In a saucepan, heat sugar and water until melted and it begins to caramelize. Add the butter and combine.
4. Add the combined flour and milk to the saucepan, stirring continuously. Boil for approximately 5 minutes. Sauce should thicken.
5. Remove from heat, add in crushed walnuts and rum extract.
6. To assemble, lay one wafer sheet on a cutting board, with the waffled edge facing up. Spread caramel and walnut sauce evenly across the top of the wafer, from edge to edge. Top with another wafer, waffled edge again facing up, and repeat layering with the cream and wafers until you end with the fourth wafer on top.
7. Cover the top wafer layer with another cutting board and weigh it down with bowls of fruit, cookbooks (this one included), anything you can find in your kitchen that'll press the wafers. Let it sit with the weight on top for 2 to 3 hours. Caramel and nut filling will harden.
8. To serve, cut into your favorite shape, and do your best to resist breaking apart the layers and eating them like an Oreo®.

MINCIUNELE PUFOASE {bowtie donut}

MAKES 8 COOKIES

You're going to laugh, but the direct translation of Miniciunele Pufoasa is "fluffy lies." I'll tell you what, if all lies are this fluffy and sweet, I don't want to ever tell the truth again. The star of this dessert is—as the translation indicates—how fluffy each donut-esque piece is. It's not necessarily sweet, but is traditionally eaten dipped in either granulated or powdered sugar.

3	eggs
2 T	unsalted butter
1 T	granulated sugar
1 t	lemon zest
3 T	sour cream
1 c	milk
4 c	all-purpose flour
1 t	baking soda
1 t	lemon juice
	oil for frying

1. In a small bowl, beat the eggs together until they begin to foam. Add in melted butter, sugar, lemon zest, sour cream and milk.
2. Add flour to the bowl, but don't mix just yet.
3. With the back of a spoon, create a little canyon in the flour. Add your baking soda to this canyon and top with the lemon juice. Mix all the ingredients in the bowl together until a stretchy dough is formed.
4. On a floured surface, roll dough out until it's approximately ¼" thick.
5. Using a butter knife, cut into strips about 2½" wide. Then cutting in the opposite direction and at an angle, cut the dough again at 3" width so that each piece resembles a diamond or rhomboid.
6. Cut a slit into the center of each rhomboid down the long way.
7. Pass one tip through the slit and turn it upside down.
8. Once each piece has been cut and flipped, let dough rest for 30 minutes.
9. Heat oil over a high flame in a deep pot.
10. Add donuts to the oil, cooking for 2 to 3 minutes on either side. Transfer to a paper towel lined plate and allow to cool before serving.

NOTE

If it's been a while, and you've forgotten what a rhomboid looks like, here's a helpful diagram, also showing how to make the slit down the middle.

COARNE CU CREMĂ {cream horns}

MAKES ABOUT 20 HORNS

A staple of Romanian weddings, these cream horns start with the lightest, flakiest pastry and are filled with a dense, decadent and oh-so-milky cream. Each bite is balanced and keeps you coming back for more. It's easy to down two, five, ten of these at once.

FOR THE DOUGH

32 T	unsalted butter
2 T	vegetable shortening
1 T	granulated sugar
2	egg yolks
4½ c	all-purpose flour
1 c	water

FOR THE FILLING

2 c	milk
⅓ c	all-purpose flour
16 T	unsalted butter
1 c	vegetable shortening
½ t	kosher salt
1 t	vanilla extract
4 c	powdered sugar

AT LEAST TWO HOURS BEFORE STARTING RECIPE

Add butter, shortening, and sugar to the bowl of a stand mixer and mix until combined and fluffy. Slowly add in the egg yolks, and then the flour and water. Wrap ball of dough in plastic wrap and allow to chill in the refrigerator for at least 2 hours.

1. Preheat your oven to 350°F.
2. Roll a quarter of the dough from the bowl onto a floured surface and roll out until it's about ⅛" thick. But into ½" wide and 10" long strips. Wrap the strips around cream horn molds (or see note). Repeat with remaining dough.
3. Bake for about 15 minutes, horns should begin to brown.
4. Allow to cool — but not completely — before removing them from the molds. Once they're off the molds, cool completely.
5. While horns are continuing to cool, begin the filling by heating the milk and flour in a saucepan, whisking constantly. Cook until it thickens, about 10 minutes, and then remove from heat and cool.
6. Add butter, shortening, and salt to the bowl of a stand mixer, and combine until fluffy. In 1 cup increments, slowly add in the powdered sugar.
7. Add milk mixture and vanilla extract and mix until well-combined.
8. Transfer cream to a piping bag and fill each horn completely.

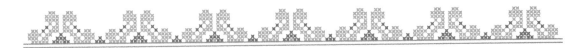

NOTE

If you don't happen to have cream horn molds laying around your house, you can fashion your own together by wrapping aluminum foil around a clothes pin.

DOBOS TORTE {chocolate and caramel layered cake}

MAKES 1 SHEET CAKE

My family is from a small village on the Romania-Hungary border, so many recipes bear a heavy Hungarian influence. This Dobos Torte *is one of those recipes, named after Hungarian chef* József C. Dobos, *who knew the perfect way to layer cake and cream.*

FOR THE CAKE

1	egg white
1 c	powdered sugar
8	eggs
½ t	kosher salt
1½ c	all-purpose flour

FOR THE CREAM

6¼ c	heavy cream
8 T	cocoa powder
⅔ c	powdered sugar

FOR THE QUICK GANACHE

½ c	dark chocolate chips
1 T	extra virgin olive oil

FOR THE CAKE

1. Preheat oven to 400°F.
2. In a mixing bowl, separate the white from the yolk of one egg. Discard yolk. With either a stand or hand mixer, whip the egg white for a couple of minutes.
3. Gradually add in sugar and continue mixing until soft peaks form. Set to the side.
4. In another bowl, beat the 8 whole eggs with the salt.
5. Fold the egg yolks into the fluffy egg white and sugar peaks. Mixture shouldn't be fully combined. You don't want to over mix.
6. In ¼ cup increments, add the flour to the bowl, continuing to fold into the egg mixture until fully combined.
7. Line a rimmed baking sheet with parchment paper. Since this is a layered dessert, you'll either have to work in batches, or cook multiple trays at once. Spread evenly from edge to edge of the pan. Layer should be thin.
8. Bake each layer for 5 to 10 minutes. Keep a close eye on the cake, as it can easily burn.

FOR THE CREAM

1. Beat the heavy cream until stiff peaks form. Be careful not to over mix and make butter.
2. Add cocoa powder and powdered sugar, mixing with a spatula until fully mixed.

TO ASSEMBLE

1. After all cake layers have baked and cooled, it's time to begin assembly.
2. Start with the first layer of cake. Spread cream evenly. Top with a layer of cake.
3. Repeat layering of cream and cake until you end with a layer of cake on the top.
4. To make the ganache, melt chocolate chips in the microwave for approximately 30 seconds. Add olive oil to help it spread.
5. Cover the top cake layer with the ganache, then move to the refrigerator to chill for at least 1 hour or until the cake and ganache sets.
6. Cut into squares and enjoy!

HIDDEN VILLAGE IN THE CARPATHIAN MOUNTAINS

PLĂCINTĂ CU MERE {apple "pie" cake}

MAKES ONE 9X9" CAKE

Even though the direct translation of this recipe is pie with apple, *it definitely falls more within the cake family than the pie family. Romanian's have perfected the ability to get those same bright and warm apple pie flavors packaged neatly in a three-layered cake: cake, then apple, and more cake. Really, the pieces of this puzzle come together in perfect harmony, in a way that'll keep you from missing your traditional apple pie. It reminds me of grandma's house—she was always the one to make this for me—and who doesn't like grandma's house?*

FOR THE CAKE

8 T	unsalted butter
1 c	sour cream
½ c	granulated sugar
2 t	vanilla extract
1	zest and juice of orange
3½ c	all-purpose flour
2 t	baking powder
⅛ t	salt

FOR THE FILLING

4	apples
½ c	granulated sugar
1 T	ground cinnamon
3½ T	unsalted butter

BEFORE BEGINNING THE RECIPE

Leave the butter out until it softens, about an hour.

1. In a large bowl, combine butter, sour cream, sugar, vanilla extract, and the zest and juice of one orange In another bowl, combine the flour, baking powder and salt.

2. Slowly add dry mixture to the wet mixture, kneading until dough is combined and elastic when stretched out. The dough will *knead* a little love to work the dry ingredients through it. (That pun was very much intended.) Dough too dry? Add a splash of water. Too wet and sticky? A little more flour should do the trick. Both should be added in tablespoon increments.

3. Divide dough into two equal pieces and form into a ball. Wrap both with plastic wrap and move to the refrigerator, chilling for at least 30 minutes.

4. While dough is chilling, wash and then grate apples using the side with the large holes. I prefer to leave the skin on — it contains most of the apple's nutrients, after all — but feel free to peel the apple before you grate it, if you prefer.

5. Using a tea or paper towel, squeeze as much liquid as you can from the grated apples. You won't believe how much liquid comes out of these apples!

6. In another large bowl, combine grated apples with the cinnamon and sugar. Stir until well-combined.

PLĂCINTĂ CU MERE *continued ...*

7. Heat 3½ tbsp butter in a saucepan. Add grated apple mixture to the pan, and cook until tender, approximately 10 minutes. The mixture will look and smell like the caramel on a caramel apple.

8. Set aside mixture and allow to cool.

9. Remove the dough from the refrigerator and preheat the oven to 350°F.

10. Grease or butter a 9x9" cooking dish or baking tray. Stretch out one ball of dough so it's pressed into the bottom of the dish, covering the dish from edge to edge. With a fork, prick it all over. Cook for 30 minutes. If you have two dishes of the same size, that will fit side-by-side in your oven, you can cook both pieces of dough at the same time. If not, I like to leave the second ball of dough in the fridge.

11. Allow cooked dough to cool on a wire rack while repeating step 10 with the other ball of dough.

12. Spread cooled apple mixture evenly over the bottom piece of cake while the top piece cooks.

13. When the top piece of cake is cooked, allow it to cool and then place on top of the apple mixture that's already spread over the bottom piece.

14. The traditional Romanian topping is dusted with powdered sugar, but can you imagine the variations you can try? Drizzled homemade caramel with crushed walnuts, a cinnamon and sugar crumble, a layer of thin-sliced apples . . . the options are endless!

15. Cut into squares to serve and enjoy!

NOTE

I used Honeycrisp apples in my baking, as they're my personal favorite, however you can choose the apple variety you like best, including Granny Smith, for a more traditional American apple pie flavor profile.

CHEC {marble pound cake}

MAKES 1 LOAF

Sometimes simple is best, but in no way does simple have to mean boring. Think of it as a canvas of possibilities. With both chocolate and vanilla flavors, you can customize it to your tastes with additions to the batter like nuts or dried fruit, or with a thick, drippy ganache poured right on top. It's a very popular cake in Romania—no special occasion necessary for this one!

4	eggs (separated)
1 T	vanilla extract
1 c	vegetable oil
¼ t	kosher salt
2 c	granulated sugar
1 c	milk
2 c	all-purpose flour
2 T	baking powder
4 T	unsweetened cocoa powder
1	zest of lemon

1. Preheat oven to 350°F and spray a large loaf pan with cooking spray.
2. Add egg yolks, vanilla and vegetable oil to a large mixing bowl. Combine using a hand mixer or stand mixer.
3. In a medium bowl, mix together the egg whites, salt and sugar.
4. Slowly add milk, flour and baking powder to the egg yolks mixture in the large bowl. Continue to mix until well combined.
5. Add in the egg whites and lemon zest and mix until fully combined.
6. Using two smaller bowls, divide the batter evenly.
7. Mix cocoa powder into one of the bowls.
8. Alternate adding the two batters (one chocolate, the other vanilla) into your large loaf pan. Run a butter knife through the batter in swirls, creating the marbled appearance.
9. Bake cake for 50 minutes, or until toothpick test comes back clean.
10. Let cake sit for 10 minutes before removing from pan. Allow to cool completely before enjoying.

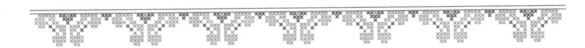

TURTĂ DULCE *{ginger bread cookies}*

MAKES 24 COOKIES

Turtă Dulce are little Christmas hugs. These mini cakes are soft, fragrant and scream of winter, perfect for those cold, snowy days where the nights are long, your tea or coffee is warm, and all you want to do snuggle up with a good book and warm blanket.

FOR THE COOKIE

1⅓ c	light brown sugar
½ c	water
2 t	warm spice mix (see note)
4 c	all-purpose flour
⅛ t	salt
½ t	baking soda
1	egg
3½ T	butter
1	zest of lemon

FOR THE GLAZE

1	egg white
1 c	powdered sugar
2 T	water

1. In a large pot, caramelize 1 tablespoon of the sugar until it becomes a darker shade of brown. At the same time, in another small pot bring the water to a boil.
2. When sugar has caramelized, pour in the boiling water, stirring as the sugar melts. Once the sugar has dissolved, add in the remaining sugar and warm spice mix and stir until the sugar has dissolved. Remove from heat.
3. Immediately add 1 cup of flour and mix with a spatula until no clumps remain. Allow to cool completely.
4. Preheat the oven to 350°F.
5. In a large mixing bowl, combine remaining flour, salt and baking soda. Add to the pot with the caramelized sugar and flour mixture.
6. Add the egg, butter, and zest of one lemon to the pot. Using your hands, combine the ingredients until the dough becomes elastic.
7. Prepare a baking tray with parchment paper. Use about 2 tablespoons worth of dough to form small balls in the palm of your hand. Place cookies on the baking tray with about an inch between balls.
8. While working, cover the balls with a damp paper towel to keep them from drying out.
9. Bake for 20 minutes, checking at 10 minutes. Cookies are done when they're lightly browned and still soft to the touch. Remove from the oven and begin working on the glaze as the cookies cool.
10. In a bowl, whisk the egg white until it becomes foamy. Add in the powdered sugar and continue to whisk until the foam looks glossy. Add in the 2 tablespoons of hot water and mix.
11. With a container that has a lid, place 5 - 10 cookies with a few spoonfuls of the glaze. Seal the lid and give the container a good shake. Repeat until all cookies have been glazed.
12. Cookies will have hardened as they cooled, and the glaze will create a thin shell of sugar on the outside, but will remain perfectly fluffy on the inside.

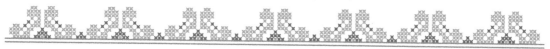

NOTE

To make the homemade warm spice mix, combine 3 teaspoons of ground cinnamon, 1 teaspoon of ground nutmeg, 1 teaspoon of ground ginger, ¼ teaspoon of ground coriander, and ⅛ teaspoon of ground black pepper.

PASCĂ {Easter bread}

MAKES 1 CAKE

Pască *is tradition for Romanians of the Eastern Orthodox faith, and is made every, well . . .* Pască! *Or, Easter. Many cultures have their own interpretation of this treat, which is inspired by the Jewish holiday of* Pesach. *The bread itself has hints of sweet, and would be perfect with a honeyed cream cheese or your favorite fruit preserves.*

FOR THE DOUGH

1 c	milk
2 t	active dry yeast
⅓ c	granulated sugar
4 c	all-purpose flour
2 T	unsalted butter
3	eggs
1	zest of lemon
1 t	vanilla extract
1 t	salt
1	egg yolk
	sugar in the raw

1. In a small saucepan, heat milk over a low flame, milk should not boil. Mix in yeast and sugar, set aside for approximately 10 minutes. Mixture should bloom and look foamy.
2. In a large bowl, add sifted flour, 3 eggs, lemon zest, vanilla extract, salt, and softened butter. Mix until well combined.
3. Add in the bloomed milk and continue to knead the dough together for at least 5 minutes. Dough should be elastic but not necessarily sticky. If it's too sticky, add in flour by the tablespoon until it no longer sticks to your hands.
4. Cover the bowl with plastic wrap and leave in a warm part of your house for at least 2 hours. Dough should double in size.
5. Preheat oven to 375°F.
6. Line a bundt cake pan with greased parchment paper.
7. Transfer dough ball to a floured surface and divide into three equal balls. Roll balls of dough between the palm of your hand and your floured surface until they become three long ropes, about 30 inches long.
8. Braid the three dough ropes together and place in your bundt cake pan. Connect the two ends of the braid together. Allow dough to rise covered for another 30 minutes.
9. Create an egg wash by mixing 1 egg yolk with a splash of water. Brush along the top edge of the dough then sprinkle with sugar in the raw.
10. Bake for 40 minutes. Cake should become an even golden brown.
11. Remove from the oven and cool lifting cake from the pan via the parchment paper, and serve.

ALBĂ CA ZĂPADA {snow white cake}

SERVES 10 - 12 SLICES

A Romanian's response to Costco's famous sheet cake. Thin, tender layers of cake between a thick, decadent cream filling allows each bite of this cake to melt in your mouth.

FOR THE CAKE

2	eggs
10 T	granulated sugar
10 T	milk
10 T	vegetable oil
⅛ t	pinch of salt
1 t	baking soda
½	juice of lemon
4 c	all-purpose flour
	sweetened coconut flakes (optional)

FOR THE CREAM

8 T	all-purpose flour
6 T	powdered sugar
1	zest of lemon
14 T	unsalted butter
4¼ c	milk
1 t	vanilla extract

FOR THE CAKE

1. Add eggs, sugar, milk, and oil to a large mixing bowl. Whisk until combined and sugar has dissolved.
2. Add a pinch of salt and then mix.
3. In a smaller bowl, neutralize the baking soda by mixing it with the juice of half a lemon, then add to your large mixing bowl. Lightly whisk to combine.
4. In one tablespoon increments, add your flour to the bowl, whisking after each addition. As you continue to add the flour, you'll notice the batter will thicken to a dough. Once this happens, it's helpful to switch from the whisk to using your hands to continue mixing. The dough should be thick and smooth, but not hard or sticky.
5. When the dough no longer sticks to your hands, form it into a ball and remove from the bowl to a floured surface. Give it a few good kneads, and add any remaining flour if it begins to stick.
6. Shape into a ball and let it rest on your counter for half an hour.
7. After the half hour has passed, preheat the oven to 350°F and divide the dough into three equal balls.
8. Place one dough ball on a sheet of parchment paper. Start by flattening it with the palm of your hands into a rounded square shape. Dust the dough and a rolling pin with flour, and continue to flatten until it becomes a very thin sheet.
9. Place parchment paper with dough on the back of a rimmed baking tray, and prick the surface of the dough with a fork.
10. Bake for approximately 15 minutes. Dough should be lightly browned, and still flat.
11. Repeat steps 8 through 10 with the remaining two dough balls.

FOR THE CREAM

1. Add flour, sugar, and lemon zest to a saucepan. Give it a quick mix with a whisk.
2. Slowly pour milk into the saucepan, little by little, whisking after each addition. Add enough milk to make a thick cream and whisk away lumps. Add vanilla extract and mix well.

ALBA CA ZAPADA *continued...*

TO ASSEMBLE

1. Line a tray with plastic wrap, and place the first layer of your cake onto it. Pour cream over the cake in a thick and even layer, all the way to the edges.

2. Add your second layer of cake on top of the layer of cream, and cover again with a thick, even layer of cream. Add the third and final layer of cake, carefully pressing together the layers so that they don't break. Cover with a thin, but even, layer of however much cream remains.

3. Sprinkle sweetened coconut flakes (optional) on top.

4. Pull the plastic wrap tightly over the top of the cake, and rest a cutting board over the entire cake to weigh it down, so that the layers can better combine. Let cake chill in the refrigerator for at least 6 hours, though overnight is ideal.

5. Let cake return to room temperature before serving.

MÂNCARE FOR THOUGHT . . .

Don't like coconut? Feel free to replace it with chopped nuts, a chocolate drizzle, fresh fruit, etc . . . The coconut flakes give the cake it's snow-like appearance, but it's just as delicious and snow white if you leave it off, too.

TORT DE BISCUIȚI *{biscuit cake}*

MAKES ONE 8" CAKE

My husband likened this to a chocolate lasagna mixed with the texture of a tiramisu, and he's pretty accurate on both counts. The layers of biscuit and cream are a lot like a traditional Italian lasagna, and because the biscuits are so porous, they absorb some of the cream and become soft, cakey bites. Yum!

2 T	hot water
2 T	instant coffee
16 T	unsalted butter
2 T	granulated sugar
3 T	cocoa powder
½ c	heavy cream
1 lb	rectangular tea biscuits, I used *Ulker Tea Biscuits*

1. In the microwave, heat water in a small bowl and then dissolve the instant coffee.
2. With a stand or hand mixer, whip together butter and sugar until creamy. Add in the cocoa powder and dissolved instant coffee, and combine. Cream should be spreadable. If it's too thick, mix in milk by the tablespoon until a creamier consistency.
3. To assemble the cake, heat a ½ cup of heavy cream in the microwave, approximately half a minute.
4. Line an 8" pan with aluminum foil. You can use any sized pan, but please note that it'll change how many biscuits and cream you'll need to assemble the cake.
5. Dip one side of the biscuit cookie into the warm milk, leaving the other side dry. Place dry side face down into your pan. Repeat process until the entire bottom of the pan is covered with biscuits. Biscuits can overlap one another if they're not a perfect fit for your pan.
6. Add a thin layer of cream mixture over the biscuits layer, corner to corner, edge to edge.
7. Repeat steps five and six until you've used up all the cream and have ended with a layer of biscuits on top.
8. Refrigerator for at least 2 hours, or until the cream has set.
9. To serve, cut into narrow, rectangular pieces.

PANDIȘPAN CU FRUCTE {sour cherry coffee cake}

MAKES 30 SQUARES

The beauty of this cake is it's meant to utilize whatever fruit is in season, which means during the Summer months it could be blueberry, strawberry, raspberry, or—my personal favorite, and what's used in this recipe—the sour cherry. Sour cherries are a very common ingredient in Romania, and popular to use as the fruit feature of this cake. And, as with any coffee cake, it's best enjoyed with a warm cup of coffee . . . yes, even during the Summer!

1½ c	unsalted butter
2 c	powdered sugar
2 T	honey
1	zest of lemon
1 T	vanilla extract
5	eggs
3⅓ c	all-purpose flour
¼ t	kosher salt
1 t	baking powder
2 lbs	sour cherries

1. Preheat oven to 350°F.
2. In a stand mixer bowl, combine softened butter, powdered sugar, honey, zest of one lemon, and vanilla. Mix together on low speed until sugar combined, then increase the speed to high for 3 minutes.
3. Add eggs to the mixer and decrease speed to medium.
4. In a small bowl, add sifted flour, salt, and baking powder.
5. In ¼ cup increments, begin to add the flour to the wet ingredients, decreasing the speed to low until the batter becomes smooth.
6. Cover a 12x16" baking pan with greased parchment paper.
7. Pour half of the batter into the pan, on the parchment paper. Add half of the cherries, sprinkled across the batter.
8. Pour the remaining batter into the pan, and top with the remaining fruit.
9. Bake for 30 to 35 minutes. The cake should be an even golden brown, and should pass the toothpick test by coming back clean.
10. Allow to cool before dusting with powdered sugar and serving in square slices.

MÂNCARE FOR THOUGHT . . .

Consider making this cake boozy by replacing your standard sour cherries with the alcohol-soaked sour cherries from my Vișinată recipe (page 220). Sure, the alcohol will cook off, but it'll leave behind a delicious brandy aroma.

SAVARINE *{rum cake stuffed with cream}*

MAKES 3 - 4 CAKES

Something soaked in rum can't be bad . . . right? Savarine is one of my mother's personal favorites, and a great alternative to a traditional birthday cake, just be careful with the candle flame, as the rum isn't cooked off in the final product. This cake is light, fluffy, and oozes with homemade cream. Please note: because the cake is alcoholic in nature, it is not suitable for those under 21 years old.

FOR THE CAKE

5 oz	milk
2 t	active dry yeast
1 T	granulated sugar
2 c	all-purpose four
2	eggs
2	egg yolks
2 T	unsalted butter
¼ t	salt

FOR THE RUM SOAK

3 c	water
1½ c	granulated sugar
½ c	dark rum
2 t	orange zest

FOR THE FILLING

2 c	whipping cream
2 T	powdered sugar
⅛ t	vanilla extract
2 t	lemon zest

1. In a small saucepan, heat milk over a low flame, milk should not boil. Mix in yeast and sugar, and set aside for approximately 5 minutes.
2. In a large mixing bowl, combine flour, whole eggs, egg yolks, melted butter and milk mixture. Stir until it becomes a smooth batter, then mix in salt.
3. Cover bowl with plastic wrap and allow to rest on the counter for approximately 30 minutes. Batter should double in size.
4. While waiting, begin the syrup. Add water and sugar to a saucepan and bring to a boil. Once sugar has dissolved, add rum and orange zest, continuing to cook for 2 minutes. Remove from heat and let cool completely.
5. Preheat the oven to 350°F.
6. Grease your 4" cake pans fill each to about ¾ full. Let rest for another 15 minutes to allow the dough to rise, filling the remaining ¼ of the cavity. Bake in batches, depending on how many 4" cake pans you own.
7. Bake for 45 minutes, checking at 25 minutes. If cake is already an even golden brown, cover with aluminum foil and continue baking. After 45 minutes, toothpick test should return clean. Allow to cool completely before removing from pan.
8. While waiting, begin the filling. In a stand mixer bowl, combine whipping cream, sugar, vanilla, and lemon zest. Whip until cream thickens and stands with stiff peaks.
9. With the cakes cooled, remove them from the pan and cut a "lid" by placing them on their sides and slicing approximately 1" from the top. Don't cut all the way through.
10. Soak each cake in the rum syrup for at least 1 minute.
11. Add whipped cream to a piping bag and pipe inside the two layers of cake. The more the merrier. Pipe a dollop on top of the cake, and finish with an optional maraschino cherry.
12. Cool in the refrigerator for at least an hour before enjoying.

BILUȚE CU ROM {rum balls}

MAKES 20 RUM BALLS

Sometimes the holidays just need a little booze. In keeping with the rum recipe trend, these balls are perfect (or perfectly dangerous) to pop in your mouth and melt into chocolate-rummy goodness. And, as with the Savarine on the previous page, the rum in this recipe is not cooked out, so please consider it an adults-only dessert.

FOR THE TRUFFLE

⅔ c	walnuts
53	animal crackers
1 c	unsalted butter
½ c	heavy cream
1¾ c	powder sugar
1 c	unsweetened cocoa powder
3 T	dark rum
1 t	vanilla extract

OPTIONS FOR THE TOPPING

cocoa powder
granulated sugar
crushed walnuts
coconut flakes

1. Preheat oven to 350°F.
2. Roast walnuts on a baking sheet for approximately 8 minutes. They should become fragrant and lightly browned. Allow to cool before pulsing in a food processor until finely chopped.
3. Add walnuts to a large mixing bowl.
4. Pulse animal crackers in the food processor until ground to a fine powder. Add to the bowl with the walnuts.
5. In a small sauce pot, bring butter, heavy cream, sugar, and cocoa to a boil.
6. Remove from heat and allow to cool before adding in dark rum and vanilla extract.
7. Pour wet ingredients into the dry ingredients and mix until well combined. If the mixture becomes too soft, chill in the fridge for 30 minutes before continuing.
8. With your hands, form mixture into 1" balls and roll them through your desired topping. I'm a fan of a little more cocoa powder, either the unsweetened variety from earlier in the recipe, or something sweet like Nesquik®.
9. Chill rum balls in the refrigerator overnight in an airtight container.
10. Enjoy cold.

MUCENICI *{honey and walnut pastry}*

MAKES 10 PASTRIES

Mucenici *are traditionally made only once a year as part of the feast celebrating the Forty Martyrs of Sebaste, which takes place between March 9th through April 23rd, but don't let that stop you from making this year round, because when you combine walnuts and honey with a dense and buttery pastry, you can't just save it for once a year!*

FOR THE DOUGH

1 c	milk
3 T	active dry yeast
4 T	granulated sugar
4 c	all-purpose flour
3	eggs
¼ c	unsalted butter
1 t	vanilla extract
1	zest of lemon
1	zest of orange
⅛ t	pinch of salt

FOR THE SYRUP

1½ c	water
¾ c	granulated sugar
1	zest of lemon
1	zest of orange
1	splash of vanilla extract

FOR THE TOPPING

½ c	honey
¾ c	ground walnuts

1. In a small saucepan, heat a ½ cup of milk over a low flame, milk should not boil. Mix in yeast and 1 tablespoon of sugar, and set aside for approximately 5 minutes.

2. In a the bowl of a stand mixer, add the sifted flour. Turn the mixer on low with the dough hook attachment. Add in each of the following one-by-one, allowing them to be mixed in fully before adding the next: yeast mixture, 2 eggs, melted butter, remaining sugar, vanilla extract, zest of one lemon and one orange and salt.

3. While the mixer continues to knead the down, slowly add in the remaining ½ cup of lukewarm milk. Mix for 7 to 10 minutes, until the dough becomes stretchy and no longer sticks to the sides of the bowl.

4. Remove the bowl from the mixer and cover in plastic wrap. Keep in a warm spot of your home for 1 hour. Dough will double in size.

5. After the hour, transfer dough to a floured surface and use your palms to lightly flatten. Divide the dough into 10 equal pieces. Keep the dough you're not working with covered with plastic wrap to keep it from drying out.

6. Roll the dough between your palm and the counter until you have a rope about 10" long and 3" wide. Twist the rope on itself and then pinch the ends of the rope together to create a ring. Finally, twist to form a figure 8.

MUCENICI *continued . . .*

7. Repeat until all the dough has been used.
8. Preheat oven to 350°F.
9. Place pastries on a baking tray lined with parchment paper and let rise for another 30 minutes.
10. Just before baking, beat the remaining egg and brush the top of the dough.
11. Bake for 20 minutes. Pastry should become an even golden brown. Remove from oven and transfer to a wire cooling rack. Let cool completely.
12. In a small saucepan, bring water, sugar, zest of one lemon and one orange, and vanilla extract to a boil, then turn down the heat to simmer for about 5 minutes. Remove from heat and strain into a small bowl.
13. Once the pastries have cooled, dip the both sides in the hot syrup, for about 10 seconds each. Return to the cooling rack. Repeat for all pastries.
14. In a small bowl, microwave honey so that it becomes more malleable.
15. Add the walnuts to a food processor and pulse until coarsely ground. Transfer to a shallow bowl.
16. Brush the honey over the top of each pastry and then dip in the ground walnuts.
17. Enjoy!

LET'S LEARN ROMANIAN . . .

Mucenici *are created to honor the forty martyred saints who died at* Lake Sevastia. Mucenici *directly translates to "saints" in English. .*

ACCORDING TO FOLKLORE . . .

There's a lot of symbolism in one mucenici. *For instance, the use of honey (bee) is meant to welcome Spring, the return of the birds to their nests and when the bees begin their work. And the figure eight shape is meant to resemble a stylized human form, a remembrance of those lost.*

There is also the "tradition" of eating forty mucenici *and drinking forty glasses of wine (or brandy), however I'm not sure how many Romanians actually practice this part.*

CREMEȘ {cream pastry}

MAKES 1 TRAY

You can't go wrong with layers, especially when those layers are light and flaky, and they're pressed together with more layers of dense, vanilla cream. Sometimes simple flavors are the best, and a recipe with a few ingredients, utilizing premade pastry dough, makes it even easier to whip out in no time!

6	eggs
12 T	granulated sugar
1⅓ c	all-purpose flour
⅛ t	pinch of salt
4 c	milk
1	gelatin packet
3 T	vanilla extract
3	pastry dough sheets
	powdered sugar

1. In a stand mixer bowl, combine separated egg yolks and 6 tablespoons of sugar, flour and salt. If mixture is too thick add in a splash of milk.
2. Add remainder of the milk to a large sauce pot and heat. Add egg yolk mixture to the milk once it boils. Stir continuously, bringing back to a boil. Cream will thicken.
3. In a small bowl, add 3 tablespoons of cold to the gelatin and rehydrate.
4. Add gelatin and vanilla extract to the cream and mix until well combined. Remove from heat.
5. Using a clean bowl for the stand mixer, whip the egg whites with the remaining sugar until it becomes a glistening foam.
6. Fold egg whites into the warm cream, careful not to over mix.
7. Set aside and allow cream to cool.
8. Bake the pastry dough sheets according to the packaging. Allow pastry to cool before assembling.
9. To assemble, place one pastry sheet on a baking tray, add a thick layer of cream to it, covering from edge to edge. Repeat, adding another pastry sheet on top of the cream, and then another thick layer of cream.
10. Refrigerate for at least three hours.
11. Finish off with the final pastry sheet. Dust with powdered sugar.

FRIGĂNELE {sweet bread in milk}

SERVES 6

A Romanian take on French toast that has been double dredged in a milk mixture first, and then egg mixture second, allowing the bread to absorb all the flavors and fry up crispy on the outside, gooey on the inside.

1	loaf of bread
4 c	milk
5 T	granulated sugar
2 t	ground cinnamon
1 t	vanilla extract
4	eggs
⅛ t	salt
	vegetable oil
	your favorite jam

1. The older the bread, the better. Trust me on this — you don't want it to be fresh, because it won't soak up the egg batter, then. Cut bread into ½" thick slices.
2. In a shallow bowl, add milk, sugar, cinnamon and vanilla extract. Mix until the sugar dissolved completely.
3. In a second shallow bowl, beat eggs and salt.
4. Heat a frying pan with oil.
5. Add one slice of bread to the milk bowl and allow to soak fully. Then transfer to the egg bowl and do the same.
6. Fry bread until both sides are a crispy, golden brown, approximately 3 minutes per side, but be diligent in checking so that they don't burn.
7. Serve immediately with your favorite jam, a drizzle of honey, or smothered in maple syrup.

MÂNCARE FOR THOUGHT . . .

A crispy bread like my Tară Pâine *recipe (page 45) is traditional, however try it with different bread varieties, like* Challah, *for example, and see which version you think makes the best* Frigănele!

PAPANAȘI {fried dough with sweet cheese}

MAKES 8 DONUTS

I challenge you to find a dessert more decadent than a donut, smothered in a sweet cheese cream and fruit sauce, which is then topped with another donut and even more sauces. No rush. I'll wait . . . In the meantime, feast your eyes (and fill your stomach) with a true Romanian treat. Let all the flavors and textures marry together in one bite—crunchy and fluffy, savory and sweet, fruity and creamy. Anyone else drooling yet?

2¼ c	cottage cheese
2	eggs
	rum extract
1⅓ T	granulated sugar
2 t	vanilla extract
2 c	all-purpose flour
1 t	baking soda
1 c	fresh blueberries
1	zest of lemon
1 t	ground cinnamon
1 c	sour cream
	powdered sugar

1. In a large mixing bowl, add cottage cheese, eggs, a few splashes of rum extract, sugar, and 1 teaspoon of vanilla extract. Use an immersion blender to blend the ingredients together. Don't blend until smooth.

2. In a small bowl, mix together the flour and baking soda. Add to the cheese mixture in ¼ cup increments. Mix until a dough is formed.

3. Flour your hands and your working surface, then transfer the dough. Knead into a ball. Dough should retain some of its stickiness, so only add more flour if you're unable to work the dough because it sticks to your hands.

4. Divide dough into 9 equal balls. Using your palm and the counter, roll 8 of the 9 balls into thick ropes, connecting the two ends together so you create a donut-like shape.

5. With the remaining 9th ball, divide it into 8 equal pieces and roll into small balls, similar to donut holes.

6. Pour enough oil into a pan so that it climbs up the edge of the pan about 2". Heat oil for frying.

7. Don't crowd the pan. Work in batches of 2 or 3. Turn the heat down and continue flipping the dough until both sides become an even golden brown. Be diligent in checking, because they burn quickly. Do the same for the donut holes. You can likely fry all 8 at once, depending on the size of your pan.

8. While dough is frying, heat blueberries in a small saucepan with the zest of one lemon, remaining 1 teaspoon of vanilla extract, and cinnamon. If you prefer a sweeter fruit sauce, add in 1 tablespoon of granulated sugar. Simmer covered on low until fruit has broken down and a sauce developed, stirring occasionally. Remove from heat and allow to cool.

9. Remove fried dough from the oil and place on a plate lined with paper towel. They will be hot, so be careful in patting them dry, trying to absorb as much of the excess oil as possible.

10. Assemble Papanași while still warm, smothering with a healthy helping of sour cream and a few spoons of your blueberry sauce. Place one of the little fried balls in the center and top off with a little more sour cream and sauce. Dust with powdered sugar.

GĂLUȘTE CU PRUNE {plum dumplings}

MAKES 12 DUMPLINGS

When you're ready to kick off the fall season you can expect fall colors, warm drinks, and— now and forever—these delicious plum dumplings, Găluște cu Prune (sometimes also called Gomboti). To me, everything about these scream fall, from the stewed and gooey plums, to the dense potato noodle that wraps it in a hug of warm, toasted flavor and sweet sugar.

4	russet potatoes
3	fresh plums
¾ c	powdered sugar
7 T	unsalted butter
1½ c	breadcrumbs
1 t	vanilla extract
4 t	vegetable oil
2	eggs
1½ c	all-purpose flour
	granulated sugar

1. Skin, cube and boil the potatoes until soft, approximately 15 minutes.
2. While the potatoes cooking, clean, cut in half and remove the pit from the plums. Sprinkle with 2 tablespoons of the powdered sugar. Set aside.
3. In a saucepan, melt the butter and fry the breadcrumbs, remaining powdered sugar and vanilla until golden brown. Stir often, as the breadcrumbs have a tendency to burn quickly.
4. Once the potatoes are cooked, discard the water and, with a stand or hand mixer, mash them together with the vegetable oil and eggs, then allow to cool.
5. Add flour in ½ cup increments until dough becomes stiff. You may need more or less flour, depending on how much water your potatoes have absorbed. Dough too dry? Add a splash of water. Too wet and sticky? A little more flour should do the trick. Both should be added in tablespoon increments.
6. Roll dough into a cylinder, and cut into 1 to 1½" pieces.
7. Take half (or a quarter, if you have a smaller section of dough) of a plum and wrap a piece of the dough around it into a plum-stuffed ball. Remember: Flour is your friend!
8. With all dumplings formed, bring a deep pot of water to a low boil. Boil dumplings for approximately 20 minutes, or until they begin to float. Don't crowd the pot. Complete this step as many times as necessary to cook all the dumplings.
9. Remove from the water and immediately dredge through the breadcrumb mixture. They should be just sticky enough to get a nice thin coating. Dust with granulated sugar and enjoy!

MÂNCARE FOR THOUGHT . . .

If you have leftover sugary breadcrumbs, don't throw them away just yet! Try making Crackly Pancakes or Waffles: add them to your favorite batter recipe and cook like normal. You can even sprinkle some on the top with some ooey-gooey syrup.

GOGOȘI {donuts}

MAKES 24 DONUTS

These delicate and aromatic donuts of vanilla and lemon are easy to make, and easier to consume in vast quantities. Unlike traditional donuts, there is no donut hole in the middle, however the dough cooks and puffs up, leaving you with a fluffy cavity in the middle—an inner donut hole, if you will. But there's no need to fill it with jelly. These donuts are absolute perfection with just a dusting of powdered sugar on top.

2 t	active dry yeast
1 c	milk
⅓c + 1t	granulated sugar
4 c	all-purpose flour
2	eggs
2 T	unsalted butter
1	zest of lemon
	powdered sugar

1. Combine the yeast with warmed milk, 2 teaspoon of granulated sugar and 1 teaspoon of flour together in a small bowl. Set aside to bloom for 5 minutes.

2. In a large mixing bowl, add egg, melted butter, remaining sugar, and zest of one lemon. Stir until all ingredients are well combined. Add yeast mixture and remaining flour.

3. Cover the bowl with plastic wrap and leave dough in a warm spot in your house for 20 minutes.

4. Transfer dough to a floured surface and roll it out until it's about ¼" thick. If it's easier, you can do this in 4 batches but evenly dividing the dough into 4 smaller balls.

5. Using a drinking glass with a diameter of about 3", cut out the donuts from the dough.

6. Pour enough oil into a pan so that it climbs up the edge of the pan about 2". Heat oil for frying.

7. Don't crowd the pan. Work in batches of five. Fry until dough until both sides become an even golden brown, approximately 1 minute per side. Be diligent in checking, because they burn quickly.

8. Remove fried dough from the oil and place on a plate lined with paper towel. They will be hot, so be careful in patting them dry, trying to absorb as much of the excess oil as possible.

9. Allow the donuts to cool before dusting with powdered and enjoying.

FURSECURI-PIERSICI
UMPLUTE *{peach cookies}*

MAKES 18 COOKIES

Oh, these peaches . . . I have dreams about these peaches. If you only walk away making one recipe in this entire book, please let it be this one. A creamy rum and apricot filling hold the two half cookies together like a surprising, velvety pit. The cookies themselves are soft, crystallized with sugar, and would otherwise melt away with each bite, if not for the core that holds them together. These cookies were always a special occasion recipe, mostly seen at weddings, so we didn't have them often growing up, but the impression they left on me has etched a never-ceasing craving on my soul. Of all the desserts in all the world, this one is my favorite.

FOR THE DOUGH

3	eggs
¾ c	powdered sugar
½ t	vanilla extract
10½ T	unsalted butter
2½ c	all-purpose flour
1 t	baking soda
⅛ t	salt

FOR THE FILLING

7 T	unsalted butter
2 T	imitation rum extract
9 T	apricot jam
11 T	whipped topping
	saved cookie crumbs

FOR THE COLORING

3½ T	water
1½ c	granulated sugar
1¼ T	cognac
1 T	yellow food coloring
1 T	red food coloring

1. Preheat oven to 350°F.
2. In a large stand mixer bowl, add eggs and turn on the machine to lightly beat. Slowly add powdered sugar to the bowl, continuing to mix. Add in vanilla extract and soften butter, mix until fully combined.
3. In another bowl, mix together flour with baking soda and a pinch of salt.
4. Switch to using a dough hook with your stand mixer, and add in the flour in tablespoon increments, allowing each to mix fully before adding more. Dough will become thick.
5. Line a baking sheet with parchment paper, and form small, 2" balls. Leave enough room between the cookies for them to expand and flatten while baking.
6. Bake for 10 to 12 minutes. Cookies should be lightly browned. Allow to cool completely.
7. While cookies are cooling, prepare the coloring syrup by heating water, ½ cup sugar, cognac in a saucepan, until sugar has dissolved. Remove from heat and cool completely.
8. Carefully handle the cookies and, using a teaspoon, scrape out the center from the flat bottom of each cookie, saving the crumbs in a small bowl. Don't scrape to the very edge of the cookie. Only about half an inch in the center should be scraped away, about ¼" deep. Set the cookies aside.

FURSECURI-PIERSICI UMPLUTE *continued . . .*

9. Crumble the cookie crumbs further, until more of a powder. Mix with melted butter, rum, apricot jam, and whipped topping until creamy and well combined. Filling won't be completely smooth because of the crumbs.
10. Spoon a heaping spoonful of filling into one of the carved out cookie pits. Press a second cookie into the filling, allowing it to hold the two halves together. Repeat until all cookies have been filled and paired together.
11. Once the syrup has fully cooled, divide it between two bowls. Fill a third bowl with remaining sugar.
12. Add yellow food coloring to one of the syrup bowls, and red food coloring to the other.
13. To dye, dip half of the cookie in the yellow bowl, pass through the sugar bowl, then dip the opposite half in the red bowl, and again through the sugar.
14. Let syrup dry before enjoying. Cookies get better with age, especially the day after baking!

LET'S LEARN ROMANIAN . . .

Piersici *(pronounced pierre-ss-each) means peach in English, but we traditionally use apricot jam as the filling in this recipe. Apricot in Romanian is* caisă *(pronounced k-eye-ee-suh).*

MÂNCARE FOR THOUGHT . . .

To make these look even more fruit-like, decorate with a mint or flower leaf placed between the two halves of cookie.

TRANSFĂGĂRĂȘAN ROAD

BĂUTURI

{bottle}

ALBUL ROMÂNESC {white Romanian}

MAKES 2 DRINKS

An adult banana milkshake makes for the best kind of milkshake, right?

3 oz vodka

1½ oz Kahlua® coffee liqueur

1 oz banana liqueur

3 oz milk

banana slices

1. Pour vodka, Kahlua and banana liqueur into cup with ice. Top with milk and a thinly cut banana slice. Stir and serve.

VIŞINATĂ {sour cherry brandy}

MAKES ABOUT 6 CUPS

Although this recipe has an idle time of at least one month, it's well worth the wait. The sugar pulls out the juice from the sour cherries, and the longer you wait, the longer the alcohol continues to work its magic. This isn't a mixing brandy—don't cover its aromatic flavors by using it in an Old Fashioned. Instead, it's the perfect post-dinner digestif to sip on, and the cherries make for the best dessert.

5 cans sour cherries
5 c granulated sugar
750 mL 150-proof white rum

1. In a large jar, alternate between layering the cherries and the sugar. Start with one can of cherries and cover in 1 cup of sugar. Repeat until both have been used. It's fine if the cherries contain their pit.

2. Let the jar sit for at least 2 weeks, until you can see that the sugar has pulled the juice out of the cherries. Each day you should see the liquid in the jar growing.

3. Add in the whole bottle of 150-proof rum. Give it a good stir.

4. Let the jar sit for at least 1 month, though the longer, the better.

5. Remove what remains of the cherries when ready to serve. Feel free to run liquid through a cheese cloth to remove any additional cherry bits that remain.

MÂNCARE FOR THOUGHT . . .

Save the vodka-soaked cherries in the refrigerator for a boozy addition to ice cream, champagne floats, or as an alternative to a shot!

FEATURED BEVERAGE

TUICĂ {plum brandy}

It seems every Eastern European country has their own version of moonshine, whether it be *Ouzo* from the Greek Isles, or *Sambuca* from the Italian boot.

In Romanian, we have *uică*, a distilled plum brandy that should arrive with a "Warning! You're about to consume *uică*" label with each pour.

Now, don't get me wrong, it's a beloved beverage by Romanians country-wide, but those who haven't grown up with a familiarity with the beverage, it can be a little hard to swallow . . . pun absolutely intended.

This is not a sipping spirit by any means. *uică* is a very much *throw it back* shot, dubbed Romania's *White Lightning* for a reason. (And that reason being because you want to get it down your gullet as quickly as possible, like a lightning strike.)

Plums are plentiful in Romania, so there's no surprise their uses evolved into fermenting and distilling, and a good *Țuică* is made from just two simple ingredients: 1. the aforementioned plums, and 2. yeast.

If you ever find yourself in the presence of *uică*, you can't not try it. (How's that for a double negative?) Grab a glass, make some solid eye contact, and cheers *noroc*!

WHISKEY CU CHASER DE MURĂTURI {whiskey with pickle chaser}

MAKES 1 DRINK

Okay, okay . . . so this isn't as much a recipe as it is a very common combination you can find in Romania. It may sound weird—acidic pickles with alcohol, what?—but you'll be surprised and amazed with the harsh burn of the whiskey is immediately mellowed-out and made way better with the addition of the pickle to follow.

1.5 oz whiskey

pickle slices

1. Pour the whiskey into a shot glass.
2. Prepare a slice or two of pickle.
3. Take shot and immediately eat pickle after.

MÂNCARE FOR THOUGHT . . .

Use the pickles from our Castraveți Covăsiți *recipe (page 84) for the true Romanian experience.*

CAISATĂ {apricot liqueur}

MAKES ABOUT 6 CUPS

Like plums, apricots are another plentiful harvest in Romania, which lends itself well to the creation of a deliciously sweet liqueur. Much like Vișinată recipe (page 220), the vodka-soaked apricots make for a delicious adult snack on their own!

40	apricots
4 c	granulated sugar
4½ c	vodka
2 T	vanilla extract

1. Washed apricots and remove the pit.
2. In a large jar, alternate layers of apricot halves and sugar.
3. Top off with vanilla extract.
4. Cover the jar and let soak for 3 to 4 days, shaking the jar every day.
5. Add in the vodka once the sugar has melted, and continue to allow it to soak for 1 to 2 weeks.
6. Remove what remains of the apricot halves when ready to serve. Feel free to run liquid through a cheese cloth to remove any additional apricot bits that remain.

MÂNCARE FOR THOUGHT . . .

Save the vodka-soaked apricot halves in the refrigerator for a boozy addition to ice cream, champagne floats, or as an alternative to a shot!

SUC DE TRANDAFIRI *{rose juice}*

MAKES ABOUT 16 CUPS

This is one of my grandfather's recipes from when he was a child growing up in Romania. As he explained it to me, he spoke fondly of its sweetness, and the hint of floral that creates a refreshing beverage on those hot Summer nights.

300 g	fragrant rose petals
19 c	filtered water
4	lemons
2 c	granulated sugar

1. Wash the whole roses in cold water before peeling the petals away from the flower.
2. Wash the lemons. Using a vegetable peeler, remove the yellow peel. Be very careful to avoid the white beneath the yellow, as it is very bitter.
3. In a small saucepan, heat the water, sugar, and peel and juice of all 4 lemons, stirring until the sugar has dissolved.
4. Remove from heat and set aside to cool.
5. Add the rose petals to the bottom of a large jar, and cover with the sugar water mixture, lemon peel and all. You may have to use a spoon to keep the petals immersed in the water, as they have a tendency to float.
6. Cover the opening of the jar with plastic wrap and place in a warm, sunny location for 2 days, mixing the jar at least twice a day.
7. The liquid should take on the color and aroma of the rose petals.
8. After the 2 days, strain the juice into another jar, through a thick sieve or colander. Keep in the refrigerator and serve on ice.

ACCORDING TO FOLKLORE . . .

It's bad luck for a bouquets to contain an even number of flowers. The superstition arose (pun definitely intended) because even-flowered bouquets were reserved for gravesites and funerals, thus giving a bouquet of 4, 6, 8, etc . . . to a friend or loved one would be seen as an insult.

Makes you wonder if the same applies to the quantity of roses are used to make the Suc de Trandafiri. You can always use an odd number, just to be on the safe side.

LIMONADA CU MIERE {lemonade with honey}

MAKES 4 SERVINGS

One beverage you'll find on most—if not all—restaurant menus, and a popular alternative to an alcoholic drink, is a simple glass of Limonada cu Miere, lemonade sweetened with honey. It's common to see entire families partaking in this delicious beverage. At first, I wasn't sure honey would make that much of a difference as the sweetener of lemonade, but it's far superior to a sugar-sweetened recipe.

5	lemons
5 T	honey
1 L	water

1. Cut lemons in half and squeeze juice into a carafe.
2. Add honey and mix with the lemon juice until honey has dissolved.
3. Add water and mix all ingredients together.
4. Garnish with lemon slices and serve chilled.

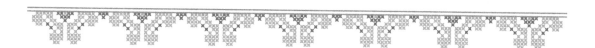

RÂȘNOV, ROMANIA

GROCERY RESOURCES

Below you'll find a list of online and storefront markets in the United States of America that provide Romanian and Eastern European ingredients. This may not include a location closer to you, so please be sure to search for your nearest market.

ONLINE

www.Fabko.com // *Specializes in the sale of food from European countries*
www.PVEuroMarket.com // *Specializes in Eastern European food and beverage products*
www.RussianFoodUSA.com // *Shop providing best European and Russian food products*

ALABAMA

European Market // *2745 Bob Wallace Ave SW Suite B, Huntsville, AL 35805*
Pofta Buna International // *2211 Seminole Dr SW - Door 14, Huntsville, Alabama 35805*
Transylvanian Romanian Cuisine // *3439 Lorna Ln, Hoover, AL 35216*

ALASKA

Eastern European Store & Deli // *W 36th Ave., #12, Anchorage, AK 99503*

ARIZONA

European Market & Deli // *4500 E Speedway Blvd, Tucson, AZ 85712*

CALIFORNIA

Continent Deli // *4150 Regents Park Row #110, La Jolla, CA 92037*
Int'l Meat & Deli // *5201 Linda Vista Rd #103, San Diego, CA 92110*
Otto's Import Store & Deli // *2320 W Clark Ave, Burbank, CA 91506*
Pacific Coast Food // *7263 Greenback Ln, Citrus Heights, CA 95621*

COLORADO

East Europe Market // *4015 E Arkansas Ave, Denver, CO 80222*

CONNECTICUT

Slavianka // *100-K Lansdale Ave., Milford, CT 06460*

FLORIDA

Balkan Grocery & Deli // *851 East State Road 434, Suite 132-134, Longwood FL 32750*
Tastes of Europe // *1811 Wiley St, Hollywood, FL 33020*

GEORGIA

Mia's European Market // *2815 Buford Dr #104, Buford, GA 30519*

IDAHO

European Delicatessen // *950 E Fairview Ave #140, Meridian, ID 83642*

Europe Delicious // *9958 W Fairview Ave, Boise, ID 83704*

ILLINOIS

Deli 4 You // *560 S Roselle Rd. Schaumburg, IL 60193*

European American Grocery & Meat // *5356 N Lincoln Ave, Chicago, IL 60625*

Romanian Kosher Sausage Co // *200 N Clark St, Chicago, IL 60626*

INDIANA

Mini Mart // *1323 S Rangeline Rd, Carmel, IN 46032*

IOWA

European Flavors // *1150 73rd St, Clive, IA 50325*

Europa Groceries // *3839 Merle Hay Rd #116, Des Moines, IA 50310*

KANSAS

European Delights // *8841 W 95th St, Overland Park, KS 66212*

KENTUCKY

European Food Market // *2221 Lexington Rd, Nicholasville, KY 40356*

European Gormet // *472 Squires Rd, Lexington, KY 40515*

LOUISIANA

Eastern European Foods Grocery Store // *3320 Williams Blvd, Kenner, LA 70065*

MAINE

Medeo European Food and Deli // *529A Main St, Westbrook, ME 04092*

MARYLAND

European Delight // *1488 Rockville Pike, Rockville, MD 20852*

Taste of Europe // *630 Quince Orchard Rd, Gaithersburg, MD 20878*

MASSACHUSETTS

Baltic European Deli // *632 Dorchester Ave., Boston, MA 02127*

MICHIGAN

American European Market // *11916 Joseph Campau Ave, Hamtramck, MI 48212*

Euro Market // *3108 Packard St, Ann Arbor, MI 48108*

MINNESOTA

Arkady's Market // U.S. 169 North Frontage Rd, Minneapolis, MN 55441

Kramarczuk Sausage Company // 215 E Hennepin Ave, Minneapolis, MN 55414

MISSOURI

Euro Market // 6936 N Oak Trafficway, Kansas City, MO 64118

MONTANA

Deli of Europe // 2173 US-2, Kalispell, MT 59901

NEBRASKA

European Grocery Deli // 2601 Champlain Ln # 100, Lincoln, NE 68521

Harvest European Market // 4451 N 26th St #900, Lincoln, NE 68521

Mediterranean Grocery // 8601 Blondo St, Omaha, NE 68134

Samovar - European Deli // 3720 N 27th St, Lincoln, NE 68521

NEVADA

Bazaar European Deli and Cafe // 3652 S. Virginia St Suite C1, Reno, NV 89502

European Delicacies // 7835 S Rainbow Blvd #12, Las Vegas, NV 89139

Eastern Market // 2550 E.Windmill Ln. Suite 160-165 Henderson NV 89074

Hungarian Market // 6380 S Eastern Ave # 6, Las Vegas, NV 89119

NEW HAMPSHIRE

Bartlett Superette // 316 Bartlett St, Manchester, NH 03102

Siberia Food Market // 100 Willow St Ste 1, Manchester, NH 03103

NEW JERSEY

Gourmanoff // 221 NJ-4, Paramus, NJ 07652

NEW YORK

Belka Deli // 8319 20th Ave, Brooklyn, NY 11214

Euro Market // 30-42 31st St, Astoria, NY 11102

European Specialties // 2142 West Genesee St., Syracuse, NY 13204

Nita's European Bakery // 4010 Greenpoint Ave, Sunnyside, NY 11104

NORTH CAROLINA

International Foods European Delights // 1636 Sardis Rd N, Ste 110, Charlotte, NC 28270

NORTH DAKOTA

Bakan Food // 2233 13th Ave S, Fargo, ND 58103

OHIO

PV Euro Market - Fine European Foods // 4805 W Pleasant Valley Rd, Cleveland, OH 44129

OKLAHOMA

European Store Oklahoma // 3604 N May Ave suite B, Oklahoma City, OK 73112

Mediterranean Imports & Deli // 5620 N May Ave, Oklahoma City, OK 73112

OREGON

Euro Market // *1950 Lancaster Dr NE # 129, Salem, OR 97305*

Imperial Euro Market // *11050 SE Powell Blvd, Portland, OR 97266*

Roman Russian Food Store // *10918 SE Division St, Portland, OR 97266*

PENNSYLVANIA

Euro Market Philadelphia // *30 South Sproul Road, Broomall, PA, 19008*

RHODE ISLAND

European Food Market // *102 Rolfe Square, Cranston, RI 02910*

Polonia Market // *736 Broadway, Pawtucket, RI 02861*

SOUTH CAROLINA

European Market // *1635 Woodruff Rd, Greenville, SC 29607*

TENNESSEE

Alesky's Market // *718 Thompson Ln, Nashville, TN 37204*

TEXAS

Borderless European Market // *1934 Rutland Dr. #500, Austin, TX 78758*

UTAH

Europa Market // *2850 S Redwood Rd A1, Salt Lake City, UT 84119*

European Tastees // *4700 900 E #51, Salt Lake City, UT 84117*

VERMONT

A Taste of Europe // *1295 Williston Rd, South Burlington, VT 05403*

VIRGINIA

Euro Foods International // *5900 N Kings Hwy, Alexandria, VA 22303*

Russian Gourmet // *907 Slaters Ln, Alexandria, VA 22314*

Troika Gastronom // *157 Hillwood Ave, Falls Church, VA 22046*

WASHINGTON

European Foods // *13520 Aurora Avenue North, Seattle, WA 98133*

Malinka Euro Market And Bakery // *9564, 18203 E Appleway Ave, Spokane Valley, WA 99016*

WASHINGTON D.C.

Eastern Market // *225 7th St SE, Washington, DC 20003*

The Mediterranean Way Gourmet Market // *1717 Connecticut Ave NW, Washington, DC 20009*

WISCONSIN

Parthenon Foods - European Market // *8415 W Greenfield Ave, West Allis, WI 53214*

ENGLISH INDEX

ROMANIAN INDEX

CLUJ-NAPOCA, ROMANIA

BÁNFFY CASTLE, BON IDA, ROMANIA

BUCUREȘTI, ROMANIA

ACKNOWLEDGEMENTS

This cookbook would not exist if not for my family, their recipes, and the reason why I am who I am . . . a Romanian through and through. You were the first to introduce me to the food I fell in love with, the recipes that make up this book.

To my sister Alexis who joined me on the journey of a lifetime to visit Romania during the 30th anniversary of the fall of communism to reconnect with our roots and the beauty of a country returning from a once stifling and oppressive era. I will never forget or take for granted our adventure, and love that we were able to do this together.

An extra and super special thank you to my husband who put up with messy kitchens and long workdays as I experimented with recipes. His tastebuds were a crucial element in the creation of this cookbook, and his honesty, love and support has only made it (and me) better. Being able to experience Romania with you, my love, by my side was an experience for the ages, and I'll never forget our first shot of authentic *țuică* and *pálinka* together.

SAPTE IZVOARE, ROMANIA

ABOUT *Ashley*

{Post-Țuică shot}

Ashley, writing as "A.M.", is a speculative fiction author who wears many hats, though she favors her dark gray cable knit beanie from Amazon, most. A descendant of Romanian immigrants, she grew up in a family that fostered all forms of creation, the guiding force which led her towards her career(s) as an author & blogger, graphic artist, and certified personal trainer & nutrition coach.

She lives in Beer & Cheese Land, Wisconsin with her real-life superhero husband, loud-mouth & drool-bucket bluetick coonhound, and *I'm-allergic-to-myself* cat.

She blogs all things Romania over at www.FromDillToDracula.com

CPSIA information can be obtained
at www.ICGtesting.com
Printed in the USA
BVHW011721260321
603512BV00007B/795